Real Estate and Taxes!
What Every Agent Should Know

VERNON HOVEN

Dearborn™
Real Estate Education

President: Roy Lipner
Publisher: Evan M. Butterfield
Associate Publisher: Louise Benzer
Development Editor: Anne Huston
Managing Editor, Production: Daniel Frey
Quality Assurance Editor: David Shaw
Creative Director: Lucy Jenkins

Library of Congress Cataloging-in-Publication Data

Hoven, Vernon.
    Real estate and taxes! : what every agent should know / Vernon Hoven.—3rd ed.
        p.cm.
    ISBN 1-4195-0298-0
    1. Real property and taxation—United States—Popular works. I. Title.

KF6540.Z9.H68 2004
343.7305'46—dc22   2004020435

Chapter 4   Applying the Passive Loss Rules to Real Estate Professionals 51

Chapter 5   Office-in-Home Rules 63

Chapter 6   Case Studies 75

Nearly 100 years ago, Oliver Wendell Holmes wrote, "Taxes are what we pay for civilized society." This may be true, but society as we know it has changed greatly over the last century, and today, people are questioning spending more on taxes than they do on food, clothing, housing, and medical care combined.

Instead, most people today lean toward the comments of Judge Learned Hand who wrote in 1934, "Anyone may so arrange his affairs that his taxes shall be as low as possible; he is not bound to choose the pattern which will best pay the Treasury. There is not a patriotic duty to increase one's taxes."

The purpose of this book is to dispel the mystery surrounding the taxation of real estate. As you read this book, you will begin to understand why real estate is a better endeavor than it has been in the last ten years, but only when the taxpayer is able to properly apply the new tax rules. It is specifically written for the real estate licensee who works with real estate investors and for the occasional users of real estate tax knowledge. It is not written for real estate tax specialists.

Although real estate licensees are not permitted to offer tax advice (unless, of course, they are also tax professionals), they are expected to have a basic knowledge of tax issues, since tax alternatives often can have a dramatic impact on the taxpayer. Chapter by chapter, this book offers numerous examples to *clarify* the issues and make them more relevant to situations real estate agents are likely to encounter.

Throughout the book, references are made by citations to the Internal Revenue Code, Tax Court decisions, Treasury regulations and rulings, and similar material, sources of information that the licensee can share with clients and their financial planners and tax professionals. These citations are extremely valuable, as they give the investor suggestions for taking substantive tax positions as proposed in this book–this is a great tool in a tax audit. Equally important, these citations save valuable research time for the tax professionals hired by real estate licensees and their investor clients.

For example, the citation [§1001(b)] refers to Internal Revenue Code section 1001, subsection b. Another citation [§1.1012-1 (a)] refers to Department of Treasury regulation §1.1012-1(a), and court cases deciding tax issues are cited as *FRL Corp. v. U.S.*

More real estate licensees are involved with residential sales than any other aspect of real estate, so it is no surprise that the book starts with the home mortgage interest deduction, which for most people is the largest tax deduction on their tax returns. The favorable tax treatment of home mortgage interest is the reason why many consumers decide to buy rather than rent.

Chapter 1—This chapter defines acquisition indebtedness and home equity indebtedness, the debts on which interest is deductible. It further explains which additional loans will qualify for this deduction and the general requirements to meet this eligibility.

Chapter 2—This chapter discusses taxation of profit, whether the sale of an investment property or the taxpayer's home. It answers such questions as what may be included in the selling price and selling expenses and takes the mystery out of the definition of "adjusted basis." Additionally, many real estate licensees are involved in the purchase or sale of options, so a discussion of how they are taxed is also included.

Chapter 3—This chapter describes various tax consequences when selling a personal residence and provides specific examples of the requirements for homeowners to use the new §121 exclusion of gain rules. This chapter answers the seemingly obvious question, "Where is your principal residence?" and explains when the capital gain is tax free. It also details what tax planning ideas are obsolete.

Chapter 4—The Internal Revenue Code contains a provision that all real estate rental activities must be treated passively (commonly known as the "Passive Loss Rules"), no matter the owner's level of personal participation, with the result that losses generated by real estate rentals cannot be used to offset active income, such as the owner's W-2 salary income or investment income, which would include interest and dividends. An exception exists for those real estate licensees who have built real estate investment portfolios. Agents who manage their own properties can deduct their real estate losses against their commission and other income with no passive loss limitations.

Chapter 4 outlines the eligibility requirements that landlords, such as real estate builders and developers, owners of rentals, property managers, and participants in the real estate brokerage business, must follow to be eligible for this deduction.

Chapter 5—Like many other Americans, an increasing number of real estate professionals conduct a major portion of their business from their homes. Accordingly, they would like to deduct a portion of the expenses associated with the home-based business on their tax returns. The new tax laws liberalize "home office" deductions, but stringent requirements must be met and proration formulas used when taking a deduction for use of a home-based office.

By properly applying the new and updated information provided in this book, most real estate licensees will benefit from these tax provisions. Their clients may also benefit when licensees properly share knowledge that might affect client decisions. At a minimum, licensees will know when to recommend that clients seek the advice of their own tax preparers.

Home Mortgage Interest Deduction

learning objectives

Upon completing this chapter, you will be able to:

- identify the two main requirements for mortgage interest deductions;

- discuss the limits on home equity loans when determining tax deductions;

- summarize the differences between acquisition debt and home equity debt;

- list the three requirements needed for deducting interest on a qualified residence; and

- summarize the general requirements that must be met for home mortgage points to be deductible.

■ Key Terms

acquisition indebtedness	interest	qualified residence
home equity indebtedness	points	secured debt

■ Overview

For most taxpayers, all mortgage interest expenses on the first and second personal residences remain fully deductible to arrive at taxable income. To qualify, the home mortgage debt must be secured by a qualified residence(s). Also, the deductible portion is limited to the taxpayer's qualified residence interest (debt incurred to buy, build, or substantially improve these qualified residences).

Interest paid for other personal expenses is normally not deductible (e.g., credit card interest, automobile loan interest). But, with proper planning, a nondeductible personal interest expense may be converted to a deductible home mortgage interest expense. To prevent abuse, some limits apply. The combined amount of acquisition indebtedness may not exceed $1 million, and the amount of home equity indebtedness cannot exceed $100,000. Calculations must be made to ensure that the deduction is permitted.

Figure 1.1 | Home Interest Deduction Formula

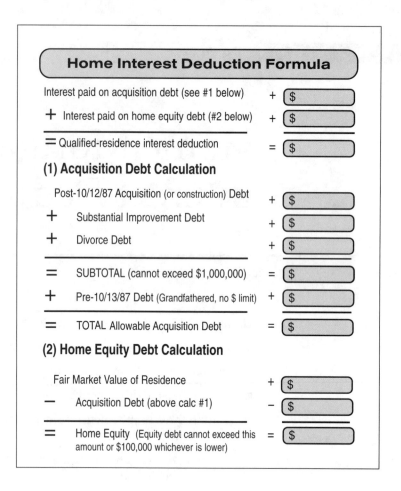

This chapter discusses the items required to calculate maximum interest deductibility, both on acquisition debt and on home equity loans. It also addresses other seemingly obvious questions, including "What is a residence?" and "Why is recording a mortgage important?"

The fill-in-the-blank formula (Figure 1.1) is used to compute the tax-deductible portion of home mortgage interest and is a starting point for defining the new terms *acquisition indebtedness* and *home equity indebtedness*. An explanation follows.

■ What Is Acquisition Indebtedness?

Acquisition indebtedness is debt that is incurred to acquire, construct, or substantially improve a taxpayer's principal or second residence and that is secured by the property.

Caps

The total amount of acquisition debt qualifying for interest deductibility is limited to $1 million for the combined principal and second residences. In the case of married persons filing separately, the total is $500,000 for each spouse. However, debt secured prior to October 14, 1987, is grandfathered and exempt from this limitation (if it has not been extended).

Reducing Indebtedness

As the amortized loan is paid off, the taxpayer's acquisition indebtedness eventually reduces to zero if the property remains the taxpayer's principal residence for the term of the loan. In other words, pay off the debt, no more interest, no more deduction.

Bill borrows $285,000 to acquire his principal residence, pays the debt down to $160,000, and wants to refinance. At this time only $160,000 can be considered eligible acquisition debt for the home interest deduction.

Refinancing

If the loan is refinanced, acquisition debt is the debt balance immediately before the refinancing. Thus, if there were no debt the day before refinancing, any interest paid on the new loan would not be deductible as acquisition debt. Only the interest expense of a loan used to substantially improve the property or home equity debt would be deductible.

Carlos purchases his principal residence for $250,000 cash. One year later, he refinances $200,000; as there is no acquisition debt at the time, it is considered excess debt, with only $100,000 eligible for home equity debt. Thus Carlos can only deduct 50% of his interest payment.

Substantial Improvements

It is not clear how much improving has to be done to be considered "substantial." In other parts of the Internal Revenue Code, substantial may mean anywhere from 15% to 35% of the fair market value. Applying those percentages to a home improvement loan on a $100,000 house could mean home improvement loans must exceed $15,000 to $35,000. Because most home improvement loans are usually less, it is possible that the loan would be considered either home equity debt limited to $100,000 or a personal interest expense and thus not deductible.

Divorce

At the time of divorce, it is not uncommon for one spouse to take out a loan to buy out the other spouse. Clearly this new second loan does not meet the requirement to be considered a new acquisition, nor is it a "substantial home improvement" loan. However, under a special provision in the tax law, the purchasing spouse's new loan is considered acquisition debt.

Figure 1.2 ǀ Allowable Acquisition Debt

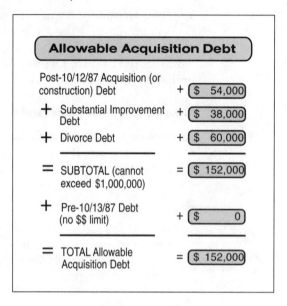

Lionel and Maya purchased a charming but very dilapidated home in 1988 for $89,000, putting 20% down and financing the balance with a conventional mortgage. With lots of "sweat equity" and the help of a $55,000 home improvement loan, they completely renovated the old place.

This year, as part of a divorce settlement, Lionel purchased Maya's interest in the home for $60,000. The home was appraised for $224,000, with a first mortgage balance of $54,000 and home improvement loan balance of $38,000, so Lionel financed the entire $60,000 and secured the debt with the home. Lionel's allowable acquisition debt is shown in Figure 1.2.

■ What Is Home Equity Indebtedness?

Home equity indebtedness is debt (other than acquisition indebtedness) that is secured by the taxpayer's principal or second residence and does not exceed fair market value of the qualified residence(s) [§163(h)(3)(C)(i)].

Lynn wants to purchase a new BMW for $75,000 and use her two residences as security for the loan in order to convert a nondeductible personal loan to a deductible qualified-residence interest loan. As shown in Figure 1.3, Lynn has sufficient combined equity in both homes to qualify for a fully deductible loan on the new car.

Fair Market Value

The price at which the property would change hands between a willing buyer and a willing seller, provided that neither was under any pressure to buy or sell, is considered fair market value.

Figure 1.3 | Home Equity Calculation

Home Equity Calculation	Prinicipal Home	Second Home
Fair Market Value	$150,000	$100,000
— Acquisition Debt	–100,000	–75,000
= Home Equity	$ 50,000	$ 25,000

$100,000 Cap

The amount of home equity indebtedness on which interest is treated as deductible qualified-residence interest may not exceed $100,000 ($50,000 for married persons filing separate returns). The amounts borrowed for educational or medical expenditures are included in this cap of $100,000.

The following is a complex home interest deduction example with accompanying table shown as Figure 1.4.

Scenario I – Mr. and Mrs. William Shearer purchased a home for $120,000 in 1972 using a VA loan. Today the home appraised for $350,000 and the balance on the first mortgage is only $600. The Shearers need money to send their two daughters to college, do additions and repairs to the property, and pay for an operation for Mrs. Shearer. They borrow $180,000 on a conventional first mortgage and pay off their old VA loan. The interest on their "acquisition indebtedness" balance of $600 plus the interest on the home equity indebtedness of $100,000 are deductible. The interest on the balance of the $180,000 loan ($79,400) is not deductible.

Scenario II – If the Shearers had an existing home equity loan of $23,000, which they used to put vinyl siding on the home and pave the driveway two years ago, they would be able to deduct only the interest on $77,000 of new home equity debt plus the balance of acquisition debt of $600. This fact of life is often a shock to the taxpayer.

■ What Is a Residence?

Generally, this includes the land and living quarters that contain sleeping space, toilet, and cooking facilities where the taxpayer normally resides (see definition of a dwelling unit on next page). But whether a specific property qualifies as a residence for tax purposes is determined by all the facts and circumstances, including the good faith of the taxpayer [§1.163-10T(p)(3)(ii)].

Figure 1.4 | Home Interest Deduction Calculation

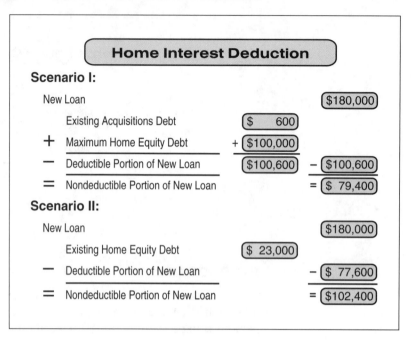

Qualified Residence

Only qualified residences are allowed a home mortgage deduction. The term "qualified residence" means the taxpayer's principal residence and/or the taxpayer's second residence [§1.163-10T(h)(5)].

Principal Residence

The home qualifying for the exclusion provisions previously mentioned is normally the home in the area where the taxpayer works. If the taxpayer is retired or not working, it is usually where the taxpayer spends the most amount of time, votes, pays taxes, files his or her tax return, etc. A taxpayer cannot have more than one principal residence at any one time.

So, does a fishing cabin in the Rocky Mountains qualify as a second residence because it has an outdoor toilet? We don't know! However, even motor homes have previously been held by the courts to be dwelling units [*R. L. Haberkorn*, 75 TC 259; *J. O. Loughlin*, DC-Minn, 82-2 USTC ¶9543r].

Second Residence

The second home, or vacation home, must (1) be a "dwelling unit" that (2) qualifies as a residence under the "use" requirements of §280A and that (3) the taxpayer elects to treat as a second residence [§163(h)(5)(A)(I),(II); §1.163-10T(p)(3)].

Dwelling Unit

A house, apartment, condominium, mobile home, boat, or similar property qualifies as a dwelling unit. A dwelling unit does not include personal property such as furniture or a television that, in accordance with applicable law, is not a fixture

[§280(f)(1); §1.163-10T(p)(3)(ii)]. This definition allows the interest expense associated with the purchase of a yacht or motor home to be deductible if the taxpayer wishes to treat the yacht or motor home as a dwelling unit.

"Use" of Second Home

For a residence to qualify as a second dwelling unit (and not a rental property), the taxpayer must either (1) not rent it out to anyone during the year or (2) personally use it at least two weeks a year or 10% of the number of days the residence is rented out to others, whichever period is greater.

Designating the Second Home

If a taxpayer owns more than two residences that may qualify as a second home, the taxpayer may designate each year which residence is to be treated as the second residence, and this election need not be disclosed to the IRS. Note, however, that this election does not apply to the taxpayer's principal residence.

Exceptions

Generally, a taxpayer may not elect different residences as second residences at different times of the same taxable year except as follows [§1.163-10T(p)(3)(iv)]:

Owning two homes and purchasing another:　If the taxpayer acquires a new residence during the taxable year, the taxpayer may elect the new residence as the taxpayer's second residence as of the date acquired.

> *Jorge owns vacation home A for the entire year, paying $3,000 interest expense. He acquires vacation home B on July 1 and pays $4,000 interest expense through December 31. Jorge may elect vacation home A as his second residence for the first half of the year (approximately $1,500 of interest) and vacation home B as his second residence for the second half of the year (the entire $4,000 of interest).*

Converting principal home into vacation home:　If a taxpayer moves out of his or her principal residence and converts it into a vacation home, the new vacation home becomes eligible as a second residence for interest deduction purposes.

> *On July 1, Jorge moves from his principal residence on St. Thomas, Virgin Islands, and purchases a principal residence in Aspen. The interest expense on his St. Thomas home is $9,000 for the year, and the half-year interest expense on his Aspen home is $4,000. If Jorge does not convert his St. Thomas home into a rental, it can qualify as a second residence for the second half of the year. The tax result is that all $13,000 interest expense is deductible.*

Owning three homes and selling one in the middle of the year:　If property that was the taxpayer's second residence is sold during the taxable year or becomes the new principal residence, the taxpayer may elect a new second residence as of that day.

Tax Tip! A residence is deemed to be rented during any period that the taxpayer holds the residence out for rental, resale, or repairs or renovates the residence with the intention of holding it out for rental or resale [§280A)d)(1);§1.163-10T(p)(3)(iii)].

> *Jorge sold vacation home A on July 1, paying $4,000 interest expense from January 1 through the sale date. He elects A as his qualified second residence for the first half of the year. Jorge also owns vacation home B, paying $7,000 interest expense for the entire year. Jorge may elect vacation home B as his new second qualified residence starting July 1. The tax result is $7,500 interest expense deductible.*

Residence Used for Business

If a residence is also used for business, the interest expense must be prorated between the residential use and the nonresidential use based on their fair market values.

> *Tom uses 10% of his residence as an office for his business. That portion does not qualify as a residence, so 10% of the interest may be deductible as business interest expense. (However, a potential problem may occur as secured debt overrides the direct tracing rules requiring Tom to deduct the 10% normal business expense as qualified-residence interest, an itemized deduction [§1.163-10T(p)(4)]. (This will be discussed in more detail later in this chapter.)*

Special Rule for "Certain Residential Rentals"

If the taxpayer rents out a portion of the principal or second residence, that portion may still be treated as residential use if

- the tenant uses the rented portion primarily for residential purposes;
- the rented portion is not a self-contained residential unit containing separate sleeping space, toilet, and cooking facilities;
- there are no more than two tenants renting (directly or by sublease) the same or different portions of the residence at any time during the taxable year. If two persons (and their dependents) share the same sleeping quarters, they are treated as a single tenant [§1.163-10T(p)(4)(ii)].

Residence under Construction

A taxpayer may treat a residence under construction as a qualified residence for up to 24 months, but only if the residence becomes a qualified residence at the time the residence is ready for occupancy. This is an exception to the basic rule that the property must be used by the taxpayer as a residence [§1.163-10T(p)(5)].

It is important to make sure that the debt is also "secured" by the residence, or this "relief" is irrelevant. If construction takes more than 24 months to complete, the interest after the 24th month and before occupancy is not deductible. The interest becomes deductible again as residence interest only after occupancy!

> *Garrison used his vacant lot, located in a recreational area, for camping privileges. It was determined to be neither the taxpayer's principal residence nor a second home inasmuch as it did not include a house, etc., containing sleeping space, toilet, and cooking facilities. Garrison's interest was treated as nondeductible personal interest [Frances B. Garrison, 67TCM 2896; TC Memo. 1994-200].*

Interest on Time-Share Purchases

Time-sharing arrangements are considered qualified residences as long as the taxpayer does not lease his or her use [§1.163-10T(p)(6)]. Therefore, swapping personal-use time-share units should not jeopardize the qualified-residence status.

Married Return

In the case of a joint return, a residence includes property used by the taxpayer or spouse and is owned by either or both spouses. Newlyweds should be careful if both previously owned personal residences and one also owned a vacation home. Individually, they did own three deductible homes but now own a principal residence and a second residence (both deductible), and one nondeductible home.

■ How Does a Debt Become "Secured Debt"?

Interest Deductibility and Secured Debt

In order for any interest to be deductible as qualified residence indebtedness interest, the debt must be secured by the residence. The debt must also be secured by a security instrument such as a mortgage, deed of trust, or land contract. In addition:

■ the qualified residence must be specified as security for the payment of the debt;

and

■ in the event of default, the residence could be subjected to the satisfaction of the debt;

and

■ it is recorded (or otherwise perfected under local or Texas state law) [§1.163-10T(j)(1); 1§1.163-10T(o)(1)].

Correct Collateral

The "specific security" requirement requires that the purchased property be pledged as collateral against the loan. Numerous taxpayers have purchased vacation homes with loans secured by their primary residences. The result is that a loan that would normally be considered acquisition debt of a second residence is now considered home equity debt of the primary residence. This is poor tax planning!

Although Mr. Singh lives in New Hampshire, he purchases a home in Georgetown, Maryland, for more than $400,000, borrowing the $400,000 from a banker. He gave the banker his New Hampshire home as collateral. Bad mistake! Because the loan must be "specific security," the Georgetown home must secure the Georgetown loan. The estimated $40,000 per year interest is not deductible by Mr. Singh, as it is personal interest.

The following taxpayer uses this knowledge about "correct collateral" to purchase personal property and still qualify for a tax deduction on the interest payments.

> *Terry purchases a $75,000 BMW on an installment contract from the auto dealer and gives his home, in addition to the automobile, as collateral. This converts a nondeductible personal interest expense to a deductible home mortgage interest expense IF the auto dealer records the house lien, along with the auto lien, with the local registrar.*

Commercial Property Pledged Against Home Loan

Borrowed money used to purchase a personal residence but secured by a commercial rental property is not properly secured, and therefore the interest is nondeductible personal interest.

Home Pledged Against Commercial Loan

Many small business owners, including real estate agents, borrow funds to purchase business equipment, such as computers, cars, office furniture, etc. Interestingly, debt of this type secured by a personal residence but used for business purposes is deductible as an itemized deduction, not a business expense.

When the security for the borrowed funds is a mortgage on a first or second home, the security, not the way the funds are used, controls the treatment of the interest. This is the only exception to the rule that interest expense is deducted by tracing how the underlying debt is used [§1.163-8T(m)(3)].

> *Dennis took out a $20,000 loan to purchase office furniture and computer equipment for his new business. The bank requires that Dennis give it a second mortgage on his personal residence as additional collateral. During the year, Dennis earns $2,400 of income on his business tax return before deducting the $2,400 interest expense he paid on the home equity loan.*
>
> *The regulation requires that Dennis report $2,400 of income but disallows the $2,400 interest expense on his business tax return. He must thus pay $367.20 self-employment tax (15.3% of $2,400). The $2,400 interest expense is deductible on his Schedule A as an itemized personal deduction. But he is still out $367.20 for self-employment taxes.*

Avoiding the Itemized Deduction

However, an election can be made to treat the debt on a qualified residence as not "qualified-residence interest" by attaching to the taxpayer's tax return a §1.163-10T(o)(5) election out of the qualified-residence interest rules. This election is effective for that taxable year and for all subsequent taxable years unless revoked with the consent of the Commissioner.

> *Continuing Dennis's example: Dennis attaches to his tax return a §1.163-10T(o)(5) election out. He traces the use of the $10,000 loan to the purchase of the business furniture and computer equipment, thereby legally deducting the interest expense on his business tax return [§1.163-8T(c)(1)].*
>
> *The tax result is that the $2,400 of income is offset by the $2,400 interest expense and therefore no self-employment tax is due. This results in a savings of $367!*

Figure 1.5 ⏐ Home Equity Calculation

Home Equity Calculation		
	Option 1	Option 2
Fair Market Value	$ 75,000	$ 75,000
— Acquisition Debt	– 45,000	– 45,000
— Business Loan	– 25,000	0
— Automobile Loan	– 5,000	– 15,000
= Home Equity	$ 0	$ 15,000

Pat's principal residence has a fair market value of $75,000, acquisition indebtedness of $45,000 (see Figure 1.5). She borrows an additional $25,000 to be used as a business loan, giving a second mortgage on her home to the lender. Later she borrows another $15,000 to purchase a personal automobile, giving both her home and the new automobile as collateral.

Without using an election to treat the business loan as unsecured, the applicable debt limit for the automobile loan would be only $5,000, the limit of her home equity amount (see Figure 1.5, Option 1). Using §1.163-10T(o)(5) election out would allow Pat to deduct all the business interest on her business tax return and all the interest on the automobile loan as qualified-residence interest (see Figure 1.5, Option 2).

Unrecorded Mortgage(s)

Sometimes, loans are not recorded, particularly when made between close family members, and by not doing so, the loan does not meet the third requirement detailed earlier when discussing "secured debt." It is also important to remember that the debt is treated as secured only as of the date on which all three requirements mentioned earlier are met, regardless of when the money was actually borrowed.

On January 1, Chuck, Sr., sells to Chuck, Jr., a lake cabin for $65,000 on an installment plan, with $1,000 down and the balance due over a 20-year contract. Chuck, Sr., does not record the sale, as he doesn't want his son to think that he doesn't trust him. Thus, Chuck, Jr., doesn't have an interest deduction on his second dwelling unit. Learning this, Chuck, Sr., records the lake cabin contract on July 1, six months later. Chuck, Jr., can deduct only the interest expense for the second half of the year.

Unsecured Liens, Mechanics' Liens, General Asset Liens

Debts secured because of a lien upon the general assets of the taxpayer or by a security interest, that is, a mechanic's lien or judgment lien that is *attached to* the property without the consent of the debtor, are not considered to be secured by a qualified residence, and thus have no value as a deduction.

■ What Are the General Requirements for Home Mortgage Interest and Points to Be Deductible?

Interest

Anything paid as compensation for the use of money is called **interest**. In order for interest to be deductible, though, there must be an existing, valid, and enforceable obligation for the individual to pay a principal sum and to pay interest on it [§163; §461].

Prepaid Interest

Cash-basis taxpayers cannot deduct prepaid interest; they are automatically placed on an accrual basis. Taxpayers may deduct interest only in the year in which the interest represents a cost of using the borrowed money. Even if paid in cash in advance, it can never be fully deducted and must be charged to a capital account and deducted in the period to which it applies [§461(g)(1)].

Martha buys a piece of property for $50,000, paying $10,000 as a cash down payment and assuming the mortgage of $40,000. At the same time, she also pays five years of interest, amounting to another $20,000. Martha must deduct the interest expense monthly over the next five years, approximately $4,000 per year. On the other side of the transaction, the seller must report the entire $20,000 as interest income in the year of the sale.

Deducting Points

Often points paid at the time of purchase or refinance are considered similar to a prepayment of interest and are treated as paid over the term of the loan. This reasoning also applies to charges that are similar to points, such as loan origination fees, loan-processing fees, or premium charges, provided that they are paid for the use of the lender's money. Such payments are viewed as a substitute for a higher-stated interest rate and therefore may be deducted over the loan term. [§461(g)].

Susannah paid $2,400 in points on a 20-year loan involving 240 monthly payments. Susannah may deduct only $10 for each payment that is due during the tax year. The remaining amount must be capitalized and deducted monthly over the remaining loan period.

Allocating Points over Life of Loan

It is often difficult for taxpayers to determine in what tax year points may be deducted when points cannot be deducted in the year paid. The IRS provides for a monthly straight-line allocation of residential points over the loan period for those taxpayers who qualify—generally, an individual cash-basis taxpayer who is charged points on a loan secured by his or her principal residence if the loan period is not longer than 30 years. See Rev. Proc. 87-15 for additional restriction on loan amounts and number of points charged.

Expenses That Are Deductible Points

Loan-processing-fee points paid by a mortgagor-borrower as compensation to a lender solely for the use or forbearance of money are considered interest. Loan-origination-fee points paid by a borrower obtaining an FHA loan are normally considered deductible interest points [Rev. Rul. 69-188, as amended by Rev. Rul. 69-582].

Expenses That Are Not Deductible Points

Charges for services, including the lender's services (such as appraisal fees, cost of preparing the note and mortgage or deed of trust, settlement fees, etc.), are not interest and therefore not deductible. They are similar to acquisition costs, even though the lender may characterize or refer to them as "points" [Rev. Rul. 67-297]. Other amounts ordinarily charged separately on the settlement statement, such as inspection fees, title fees, attorney fees, property taxes, and mortgage insurance premiums, cannot be disguised as points [Rev. Rul. 92-2].

Points, Exception

The entire amount of points paid for a mortgage note may be deducted in the year of payment if the

- loan is incurred in connection with the purchase or improvement of a principal residence and the indebtedness is secured by that home;
- payment of points is an established business practice in the area where the debt is created; and
- points do not exceed the amount generally charged in the area [§461(g)(2)].

If the loan exceeded the $1 million qualified acquisition-indebtedness cap, points paid would not qualify [Rev. Rul. 92-2; Rev. Proc. 92-12].

Susannah paid $2,400 in points on a 20-year loan involving 240 monthly payments when purchasing her principal dwelling. Because she lives in an area where points are normally charged, Susannah may deduct all $2,400 in the year of the payment of the home mortgage points.

Closing Statement Designates Points

The IRS, "as a matter of administrative practice," permits the current deduction of points incurred when purchasing a principal residence if all the following conditions are met:

1. The charges are paid for the use of the lender's money or as a substitute for a higher-interest rate.

and

2. The Uniform Settlement Statement, HUD Form 1, clearly designates the amounts as "points" incurred to procure the loan. Therefore, labels such as loan origination fees, loan discounts, discount points, points, service fee

points, and commissions paid to a mortgage broker for arranging financing are acceptable [Rev. Rul. 92-2]. Loan-origination-fee points paid by the borrower to obtain a VA or FHA mortgage are now also deductible as interest.

and

3. The points must be stated as a percentage of the principal amount borrowed.

and

4. The amount must be paid directly by the taxpayer [Rev. Proc. 92-12].

Points Paid Deductible by Buyer and Seller

When a seller pays "points" on the sale of a principal residence, the buyer may deduct those points as interest, but both must subtract these points from the sales/purchase price. Seller-paid points are viewed as an adjustment to the purchase price of the home when certain requirements are met. The pro-home-buyer rule is retroactive for points paid by the seller [Rev. Proc. 94-27; Reg. §1.1273-2(g)(5)(Example 3)].

Danny Seller sells Roberta Buyer his principal residence for $101,600 and also agrees to pay two of the four points on Roberta's new $80,000 mortgage ($1,600). Danny must decrease his net sales price to $100,000. Roberta's purchase price is $100,000, and she gets to deduct all $3,200 of the mortgage points, just as if she had paid it personally.

IRS Requirements

If the previously mentioned requirements are met (i.e., computed as percentage, established business practice, not excessive, purchase points only, and paid directly), the deductible amount designated as mortgage discount points on HUD Form 1 may be shown as paid from either the borrower's or the seller's funds at closing.

Key to Deductibility

If properly substantiated, points paid by the seller (including points charged to the seller) in connection with the buyer's loan will be treated as paid directly by the buyer from funds that have not been borrowed. This requires that the buyer receive the seller's closing statement along with the buyer's closing statement, typically not done unless the HUD Form 1 is used (HUD Form 1 includes charges for both the seller and the buyer on the same form).

Taxpayers should make sure the points are paid in cash. For points to be deductible, they must be paid from separate funds at the time of loan closing and cannot be paid from borrowed funds.

Points withheld by a lender from loan proceeds may not be deducted by the borrower in the year the points were withheld, because the withholding does not constitute payment within that tax year. Such withholding reduces the issue price of the loan, and thereby the amount of the deduction is governed by the original issue discount rules [§§1271-1274] [*R.A. Schubel*, 77 TC 701 (1981)].

Points Paid from Earnest Money Deposit

The buyer does not have to bring additional cash to closing if the earnest money deposit exceeds the cost of the points. So long as the funds are not borrowed, points may be deducted if they do not exceed the down payment, escrow deposit, earnest money applied at closing, and other funds actually paid over at closing [Rev. Proc. 92-12; Rev. Rul. 92-2].

Rental of Large Portion of Residence

Even though taxpayers may rent out a portion of their home, points used to acquire the home may be written off as principal residence points, because the Tax Court has determined that there is "no exception in Code Section 461(g) for a principal residence which is also used (partly or substantially) for rental purposes."

The Tax Court's logic should also extend to a principal residence with a home office, a situation facing many home-based businesses. A home office should not affect the write-off of the points. Note, however, that this rule would not apply to the purchase of a duplex with one unit being used personally, as that represents the purchase of two assets, a personal home and a business rental.

> *Russell rented a substantial portion (85%) of his principal residence. The points he incurred to acquire the mortgage on the residence did not have to be amortized merely because the principal residence was also partially used for rental purposes. The Court held that the points Russell paid were deductible on Schedule A under Code Sections 163 and 461(g) [Russell, TC Memo, 1994-96, 67 TCM 2347].*

Refinancing Points Never Currently Deductible

No matter how the taxpayer arranges to pay for points paid in refinancing a mortgage, these points are not deductible in full in the year paid, even if the mortgage is secured by the taxpayer's principal residence. According to the IRS, points paid to refinance an existing home mortgage are for repaying the taxpayer's existing indebtedness and are not paid "in connection with" the purchase or improvement of the home.

Therefore, taxpayers must deduct refinance points monthly over the loan period. However, if part of the proceeds from the refinancing is being used to improve the personal residence, the taxpayer may deduct a portion of the points in the tax year paid [Rev. Rul. 87-22].

> *Susannah paid $2,400 in points on refinancing a 20-year loan involving 240 monthly payments on her principal residence. Susannah may deduct only $10 for each payment that is due during the tax year.*

Advance Planning May Help

The following case illustrates a creative, preplanned approach to the purchase and renovation of the taxpayer's new home in order to deduct the points required for permanent financing.

> *James and Zenith Huntsman bought a principal residence financed by a $122,000 mortgage loan with a balloon payment due in three years. Shortly thereafter, they obtained a $22,000 home improvement loan secured by a second mortgage. Within the three years, the Huntsmans obtained a 30-year variable-rate mortgage of $148,000 and paid off the prior loans with the proceeds. When obtaining their new loan, the Huntsmans paid $4,400 in points and immediately deducted it as points paid "in connection with" the purchase of a principal residence [see the exact wording of §461(g)(2)]. The IRS disallowed the current deduction. However, the Tax Court allowed it!*

The U.S. Court of Appeals for the Eighth Circuit has stated, "Obtaining the short-term financing was merely an integrated step in securing the permanent financing to purchase the home." Judge Lay concluded that the statement "in connection with" should be "broadly construed" [*James Richard Huntsman v. Comm.,* CA-8 (rev'g TC) 90-2 USTC 9150].

The IRS has announced that it will not follow the Huntsman decision outside the Eighth Circuit, warning that the test created by the Eighth Circuit requires an examination of the facts of each case to determine whether a refinancing is sufficiently connected with the purchase or improvement of a principal residence. The IRS holds that Congress enacted §461(g)(2) to eliminate the case-by-case approach to the deductibility of points [AOD no. 1991-02].

Any fact pattern other than the facts in the Huntsman case will probably not be considered acquisition points, including refinancing to lower the interest rates [*Kelly v. Comm.,* TC Memo 1991-605, 62TCM 1406; *Dodd v. Comm.,* TC Memo 1992-341].

The Huntsmans received their current year deductibility but not without a fight, and it is not clear whether courts in other jurisdictions will agree with the U.S. Court of Appeals for the Eighth Circuit.

Other creative taxpayers should be forewarned of a possible disallowance at audit but not necessarily loss of deduction—if they are willing to go to court.

Deductibility of Points When Home Sold Prior to Loan Payoff

Whenever the property is sold or disposed of, any unamortized part of the financing expense can be charged off and deducted as interest expense. These remaining points are fully deductible in the year that the home is sold. No difference is made whether the new buyer assumes the mortgage, the property is simply sold subject to the mortgage, or the loan is paid off by the seller at the time of the sale.

> *David Seller places a ten-year mortgage on an apartment building on July 1, 2001, using the proceeds to pay off an existing mortgage and to pay for repairs and operating expenses. He pays $1,000 in points at closing, of which only $50 is deductible in 2001 ($1,000 divided by 10 years = $100 a year, or $50 for half the year).*
>
> *David sells the property on July 1, 2005. The remaining capitalized interest of $650 is triggered and becomes totally deductible as an interest expense in 2005. It doesn't matter whether the loan was paid off or property sold subject to the mortgage.*

Deductibility of Points When Loan Prepaid

If the loan is paid off in cash or its equivalent, the points become fully deductible in the year of the payoff of the loan [*B. L. Battlestein*, CA-5, 80-1, USTC ¶9225] (IRS disagrees; see PLR 8632058). Refinancing, however, will not trigger this option. The loan must be paid off in cash or its equivalent.

Seller Assistance in Obtaining Loan

A loan charge of points or a loan replacement fee, paid by the seller of a residence as a condition to the arrangement of an FHA financing term for the buyer, is not deductible as interest. This charge is viewed as a selling expense that reduces the amount realized [Rev. Rul. 68-650; Rev. Proc. 92-12A].

Mortgage Insurance Premium Points

The IRS maintains that the insurance premiums on FHA loans are insurance and not interest and therefore are not deductible as interest.

■ Conclusion

Real estate licensees should be aware that for most Americans, interest paid on loans to buy or substantially improve their primary residences remains the largest and potentially most viable way to reduce taxable income. The key is to properly use the new tax law.

As this chapter shows, many technical traps exist that can cause the homeowner to lose this valuable deduction. The material here can help homeowners and investors maintain a legal deduction in case of an IRS audit. It may also factor into decisions to buy or sell real estate based on the tax consequences.

Real estate licensees are cautioned not to offer accounting advice, unless they are also trained as tax advisers or are accountants. However, licensees should have a fairly broad knowledge of what may or may not be deductible and should know when to advise their clients to seek additional, more detailed advice.

■ Chapter 1 Review Questions

1. Home mortgage interest is not usually deductible when the loan is secured by the taxpayer's primary residence.
   a. True
   b. False

2. Normally, interest paid on a home equity loan is deductible on loans up to $100,000.
   a. True
   b. False

3. Home mortgage discount points are deductible in the year they are paid if paid by separate funds at closing.
   a. True
   b. False

4. Proceeds from a home equity loan may be used to buy a car, and the interest is deductible.
   a. True
   b. False

5. Acquisition debt may be increased when refinancing, and all the interest will still be deductible.
   a. True
   b. False

6. Once one home has been designated as the second home, it must always be the second home.
   a. True
   b. False

7. When two people who own separate residences get married, they may lose one of their deductions.
   a. True
   b. False

8. The interest payments on unrecorded home mortgages are not deductible.
   a. True
   b. False

9. Fees for lender's services such as appraisals and preparing documents are often deductible.
   a. True
   b. False

10. The maximum amount of acquisition indebtedness for both the principal and second residence is $500,000.
    a. True
    b. False

2

Taxation of Profit— How Gains or Losses Are Computed

learning objectives

Upon completing this chapter, you will be able to:

■ explain the gain or loss formula;

■ identify items that may be included in the selling price;

■ list items that may (or may not) be used as selling expenses;

■ explain adjusted basis and why correct determination is valuable in determining gain (or loss); and

■ summarize the differences between repairs and capital improvements and how this test applies differently to rental properties and personal residences.

■ Key Terms

adjusted basis	depreciation	selling expenses
capital improvement	option	selling price

■ Overview

Taxpayers must remember that whenever an asset is sold, exchanged, or disposed of in any income-taxable manner, the seller must calculate the gain or loss. Even before purchasing real property, real estate licensees and their investor clients need to be aware of the rules used to determine gains or losses. Knowledge of the rules permits advance planning that can substantially reduce taxable gain, certainly a benefit to the taxpayer.

Figure 2.1 | Gain or Loss Formula

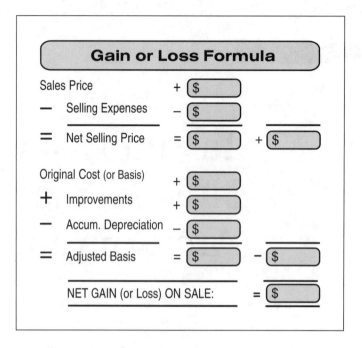

The basis of all planning begins with understanding the gain (or loss) calculation. This chapter provides a short and simple methical procedure to accurately determine the amount, even when an option to purchase is involved.

Subsequent chapters will discuss the numerous code sections that tell the taxpayer what to do with the gain or loss, how much is taxable or nontaxable, what portion of the gain may be rolled over, or what portion of the gain may be excluded.

Nonreportable Transfers

Some transfers never need to be reported. Such transfers include property received by gift or inheritance. These transfers are not taxable because no sale or exchange occurred although the giver may have to pay some gift or inheritance tax. Even money received in a refinance is not taxable . . . no sale took place.

When Dad gives Daughter the vacation cabin or Aunt Millie leaves Nephew the family plot, none of the four reports this transfer on his or her income tax return. One was a gift, the other was an inheritance, and neither was a sale or an exchange.

■ What Is the Gain or Loss Formula?

When any property is sold or exchanged, the taxpayer must inform the IRS of any gain or loss. Although the formula is simple, i.e., sale price less original price (or basis), we recommend use of the formula in Figure 2.1 to avoid any mistakes.

Figure 2.2 | Gain or Loss Calculation

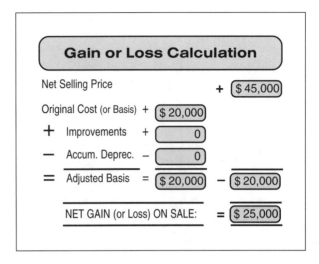

■ Computing Gain or Loss

The easiest way to demonstrate each line of this formula is by using a series of examples that become progressively more difficult.

Basic Situation

Roberta purchased ten acres of land for $20,000 and sells it to Joe ten years later for $45,000. In this overly simplified case (i.e., no selling expenses shown) Roberta's gain for tax purposes is $25,000 ($45,000 - $20,000) (see Figure 2.2).

First Variation. Roberta builds a home on the lot.

After purchasing the ten acres of land, Roberta builds a home for $150,000 and sells it to Joe ten years later for $245,000. She pays the following expenses at the time of sale: $17,150 commission (7%); $450 title insurance; $300 attorney's fee; $200 accountant's fee; $4,900 two-point origination fee; and $200 closing costs for total selling expenses of $23,200. Her net gain of $51,800 is calculated as shown in Figure 2.3.

Second Variation. Roberta rents out the home for a few years before selling it.

Continuing the previous example, Roberta lives in her home for five years, when she takes a new job in another city. She rents the home for three years, until she sells it to Joe for $245,000. During the three years she rents the property, Roberta claims a total of $16,136 in depreciation on her tax returns. Her selling expenses totalled $23,200. Her net gain of $67,936 is calculated as shown in Figure 2.4.

Figure 2.3 | Gain or Loss Calculation

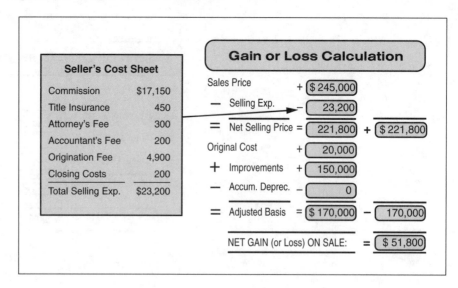

Roberta's gain increases by $16,136 ($67,936 - $51,800) over the previous example, which is the exact amount of depreciation she deducted during her period of ownership. Accumulated depreciation increases gain at the time of sale (called depreciation recapture gain) by the same amount as the prior deductions. Depreciation taken on Roberta's tax returns reduced her tax burden in those years, but the IRS makes it up when the property is sold.

Figure 2.4 | Gain or Loss Calculation

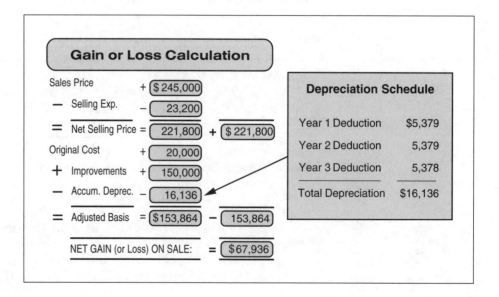

■ What Is Included in the Selling Price?

For tax purposes, the amount realized on a sale includes the amount of cash received plus the fair market value of any other property received [§1001(b)1]. For example, a seller may accept a piece of jewelry, an automobile, or some other item or service as all or part of the "value received" in the exchange. Moreover, if the buyer takes over a mortgage(s) (assumption or subject to), those amounts are also figured into the total sale price [§1.1012-1(a)].When the selling or purchase price is not specifically stated or involves more than cash, the selling/purchase price is arrived at by the following formula:

Selling / Purchase Price Formula

1. Cash down payment   +$_____
2. Cash brought to closing for selling and purchase expenses   +$_____
3. Amount received for option to buy   +$_____
4. Assumed mortgages or other encumbrances on property at face value* (whether assumed or taken "subject to")   +$_____
5. Face amount of two-party notes (e.g., between buyer and seller) given to seller (mortgage note or trust deed) or face amount of buyer's contracted promise to pay (land contract, contract for deed)   +$_____
6. Fair market value of third-party obligations (e.g., U.S. Treasury bonds, AT&T debentures)   +$_____
7. Face value of liens against property, whether or not buyer is personally liable for the liens (e.g., back taxes, etc.)†   +$_____
8. Fair market value of property (other than cash) received from buyer (e.g., diamonds, free trips, value of services rendered in exchange for the property received, etc.)   +$_____

ACTUAL SALES PRICE ‡   +$_____

* The principal part of the mortgage cannot include interest because of the imputed interest rules or the original issue discount rules [§483; §§1271-1274].
† Includes charges accrued against the property and assumed by the purchaser, such as taxes, mortgage interest, and liens.
‡ Commissions and other selling expenses paid or incurred by the seller do not reduce the selling price even though they do reduce net profit.

Contract Price v. Total Assets Transferred

The selling price for tax purposes is the total assets transferred from the seller to the buyer, whether they are or are not mentioned in the sales contract. The contract price contained in the legal documents is normally, but not always, the same as this calculation.

Juanita purchased an office building from Gary, paying him $10,000 in cash, assuming a $90,000 mortgage, and giving Gary her note (a second mortgage) for $50,000. The sales/purchase price for Juanita and Gary is computed as follows:

Selling / Purchase Price Formula	
1. Cash down payment	+$ 10,000
4. Assumed mortgages or other encumbrances on property at face value (whether assumed or taken "subject to")	+$ 90,000
5. Face amount of two-party notes (e.g., between buyer and seller) given to seller (mortgage note or trust deed) or face amount of buyer's con-tracted promise to pay (land contract, contract for deed)	+$ 50,000
ACTUAL SALES PRICE	= $150,000

Adding in Personal Property

Mary purchased an apartment building from Dutch, with a contract price of $150,000 ($10,000 in cash, assumed mortgage of $90,000, and Mary's two-party note for $50,000, a second mortgage). When Dutch started to back out of the transaction at closing, Mary gave Dutch a $10,000 diamond ring to keep the transaction together. Is the sales price $150,000 (contract price) or $160,000 (assets exchanged)?

Selling / Purchase Price Formula	
1. Cash down payment (earnest money deposit)	+$ 10,000
4. Assumed mortgages or other encumbrances on property at face value (whether assumed or taken "subject to")	+$ 90,000
5. Face amount of two-party notes (e.g., between buyer and seller) given to seller (mortgage note or trust deed) or face amount of buyer's contracted promise to pay (land contract, contract for deed)	+$ 50,000
8. Fair market value of diamond ring	+$ 10,000
ACTUAL SALES PRICE	= $160,000

Allocating Purchase Price among Properties Purchased

The buyer and seller must agree on the sales/purchase price. The IRS requires that the seller's sales price be the same as the buyer's purchase price. When a buyer acquires more than one property at the same time (i.e., land and building), the purchase price must be allocated among the properties purchased to determine the basis of each [§1060; *FRL Corp. v. U.S.*, 74-2 USTC ¶9560 (D Mass 1974)].

Possibility of Double Tax Penalty

The sales/purchase price of each component is required to be the same for both parties, and if they are not, the IRS has the power to change the allocation to the detriment of both parties. The allocation must be done in a fair and equitable manner, i.e., based on the fair market value of the different assets on the date of purchase [§1.1060-1T(h); §1.61-6 (a)].

Depreciation—A method of matching income and related expenses, depreciation recognizes the decrease in value caused by wear and tear, outdated interior improvements, and neighborhood problems. Land itself may never be depreciated, only the improvements.

Depreciable Property

Three conditions must be met before the depreciation tax deduction is allowed. Generally, depreciable property meets the following criteria:

1. It is a capital expenditure in depreciable property, that is, not inventory, land, etc.

and

2. It is used in a trade or business or held for the production of income.

and

3. It has a definite useful life of more than one year.

Mandatory Depreciation

Once property qualifies for the depreciation expense deduction, the cost or other basis of the property will be decreased for depreciation at the end of each taxable year, whether or not the taxpayer has "used" the depreciation.

Effect of Accumulated Depreciation

The increased gain in the second variation above is exactly the same amount as the accumulated depreciation. However, Roberta had no choice; she had to take the depreciation because renting out her home qualified it for mandatory depreciation (see Figure 2.4 and explanatory text).

■ What May Be Included as Selling Expenses?

Selling Expenses

All expenses incurred to complete the sales transaction may be used to reduce the selling price. In other words, if a capital gain is realized on the sale, the selling expenses reduce that gain. They are not deductible against ordinary income.

Not Selling Expenses

Prorated items such as prorated taxes, insurance, interest, and rent as well as finance charges paid by the buyer may not be counted as selling expenses. Moreover, not included are any expenses that physically affect the property (e.g., repairs or improvements), even if they are to prepare the property for sale.

> *Betty Broker instructs Manuel to spend $2,500 sprucing up his property to get it ready for sale. Is this a selling expense? No, even though Manuel would never have spent the money if Betty hadn't told him it was necessary to make the property salable.*

Examples of Deductible Selling Expenses

Any other expenditure's related to the sale other than those physically affecting the property are accepted. These include

- real estate sales commissions;
- points paid by the seller to the buyer's lending institution;
- attorney and accountant's fees;
- settlement charges;

Figure 2.5 | Adjusted Basis Computation

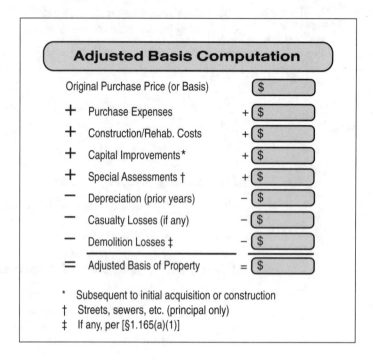

- closing fees;
- appraisal fees;
- advertising;
- escrow fees;
- title examination;
- title insurance;
- title certificate (Torrens) and registration;
- document preparation;
- recording fees;
- transfer tax stamps;
- survey; and
- pest inspection.

■ What Is Adjusted Basis?

Adjusted basis is the original cost of property (or basis, if the owner didn't buy the property), plus the value of improvements made on the property, minus depreciation and losses taken while owning it. A more extensive formula is shown as Figure 2.5 [§263; §1.263(a)-1].

Original Cost v. Basis

Usually, original cost is the cash transferred and/or mortgages created or assumed at the time of purchase. However, property is frequently transferred on a noncash basis. These include the following:

- **Inheritance:** The basis for inherited property is normally its fair market value at the time of the decedent's death [§1014].

- **Gifts:** The basis for a bona fide gift is usually the donor's basis (called carry-over basis) plus gift tax paid (if any) on the appreciation in value [§1015].

- **Spousal Transfers:** Any property received from a spouse during marriage or incident to divorce is considered a transfer by gift [§1041].

- **Exchanges:** If the property is acquired in a tax-free exchange, the basis of the received property becomes the basis of the property surrendered, less any "boot" received (i.e., money, non-like-kind property, etc.), plus any gain (or minus any loss) recognized on the deal [§1031(d)].

Adding to Basis (Purchase Expenses)

Common purchase price expenses that may be added to the basis include attorney fees [Rev. Rul. 68-528] and the following:

- Escrow fees
- Recording costs
- Accountant's fees
- Broker and finder fees
- Appraisal costs
- Surveys
- Inspection fees
- Title search and title insurance charges
- Costs of acquiring any outstanding leases
- Any expenses related to purchase other than those physically affecting the property

Purchasers, even professional investors, frequently overlook the expenses incurred to purchase an asset (usually paid after closing) when calculating their adjusted basis. They simply pay the expenses after closing and forget them. These acquisition costs may not be deducted. Not adding to the basis decreases investor's depreciation and unnecessarily increases his or her subsequent gain.

Adding to the Basis (Construction, Reconstruction, Capital Improvements)

Any money spent to improve existing property or construct new property (or rebuild if property is damaged) must be added to basis and depreciated. Currently, these "capital expenditures" may not be deducted but must be recovered through annual expenses (called *depreciation deductions*) taken over the useful life of the depreciable property [§167; §168].

Capital expenditures are generally defined as amounts paid to (1) acquire property with a useful life in excess of one year or (2) permanently improve property [§263; §1.263(a)-1].

Handling Repairs and Maintenance

Repairs on personal residences are not deductible nor can they be added to the home's basis. Homeowners would prefer them to be capital improvements, which will reduce the gain on a subsequent sale.

On the other hand, investors want expenditures on business or investment properties to be considered repairs so that the expenses may be deducted in the year they occurred, rather than depreciated. When repairs are made to maintain the property in efficient operating condition, and as long as they do not materially add to the property's value or prolong its useful life, they are not considered capital improvements.

Repairs v. Capital Improvements

If an investor answers yes to either of the following two questions, the cost is generally a capital expenditure:

1. Does the expenditure materially add to the property's value?
2. Does it prolong the property's useful life?

Casualty Losses Reduce Basis

Fire, theft, hurricane, etc., reduce basis to the extent of the deductible loss allowable to the owner. Normally, the amount of the loss deduction equals the loss in value less any insurance proceeds recovered, but the loss deduction may not exceed the adjusted basis of the property prior to the occurrence [§1016(a)(1); §1.165-7(b)-(1)]. Amounts spent after the casualty are normally added to basis, treated simply as another improvement [Rev. Rul. 71-161, 1971-1 CB 76].

■ Capital Gain Rates and Rules

For capital assets held more than 12 months and sold after May 6, 2003, the maximum tax rate on net capital gains is 15%. For individuals in the 15% bracket, the long-term capital gains tax rate is lowered to 5%.

Note: The personal exemption phaseout and the limit on itemized deductions indirectly increase the taxable income. This can cause the net capital gains to be taxed at something higher than the advertised 15% rate for a high-income taxpayer. The actual individual "effective tax bracket" experienced by net capital gains may be 17% to 20% or higher because of the 2% personal exemption phaseout and the multiple limits on itemized deductions.

■ How Are Options Taxed?

Sometimes the investor purchases an option to buy real property in the future instead of buying the property right now, usually paying only a small fraction of the total purchase price for this future right. With an option, the potential buyer can acquire the property before a designated future date without fear that the seller will sell it to someone else or raise the price. Options are often used to allow the buyer enough time to arrange for financing or to determine if he or she really wants to buy the property.

The potential buyer also retains the right not to purchase the property at all, simply allowing the option to "lapse." When this happens, the optionee-buyer forfeits the option money as a "penalty" for failure to exercise, thus compensating the seller for removing the property from the market.

Kumar, the optionee, pays Bernie, the owner, $5,000 cash for the right (option) to purchase property for an agreed $150,000 any time within the next three years. If Kumar exercises his option, Bernie must sell for $150,000, even if the value of the property has subsequently increased. On the other hand, Kumar can simply walk away if he chooses—generally done when the value of the property falls below $150,000, the option price.

Tax Ramifications of Options

The initial receipt of option money is not a taxable event to either the seller or the buyer, creating the unusual situation that allows the seller to receive cash that is not immediately taxable [§1234]. An option is a different asset from the property covered by the option and is treated much the same as a deposit [§1234; *Lucas v. North Texas Lumber Co.*, 281 US 11 (1930)]. Therefore, the option payments do not become income to the potential seller until the option either lapses or is exercised.

Tax Ramifications to the Buyer

When real property is acquired through the exercise of an option, the buyer adds the cost of the option to the purchase price. If the buyer allows the option to lapse, the buyer is allowed to deduct the option payment as a loss, subject to all the loss restrictions, but only at the end of the option period [§1234(b)(2); §1234-1(b)].

If the option relates to real property, the option is generally considered either a capital asset or a §1231 trade or business property. The character of the loss is determined by the property to which the option applies and therefore would be a capital loss or an ordinary business loss [§1.1234-1(a); §1234-(a)(1)], defined in Chapter 3.

Tax Ramifications to the Seller

If the option is exercised, the option money is included in the sales price of the property sold. If the option is not exercised, the gain is ordinary income, although dealers in options are subject to special rules [§1.1234-1].

Selling an Option

There is a real advantage to selling an option instead of exercising the option (i.e., buying and then selling the actual property). The new owner simply steps into the shoes of the old owner and exercises the option. The investor must own the option for more than 12 months in order to take advantage of the long-term capital gains tax rates.

On the other hand, when the unsophisticated investor exercises the option by buying the property and then turns around and sells it, even the next day, he or she then realizes a short-term capital gain.

On January 1, Tom purchased, for $500, a two-year option to buy a mini-shopping center having an exercise price of $300,000. Two years later, Tom receives an offer of $400,500 for the building. He is willing to claim the whole gain in the year of the sale, so Tom exercises the option for $300,000 and the same day sells the building for $400,500. This results in a short-term capital gain because Tom has owned the property for less than one day, not the required "more than 12 months."

By buying and then selling the property rather than simply selling the option, Tom converted a long-term capital gain to a short-term capital gain, not understanding that the option is a different asset from the property it is optioning.

Of course, the buyer does not care what method is used. If Tom sells him the option for $100,500, the option price is added to the exercise price of $300,000, leaving the buyer with the same basis of $400,500 as if he had purchased it directly from Tom.

■ Conclusion

Computation of gains and losses can be done simply and methodically using the gain or loss formula. However, taxpayers should pay close attention to what may or may not be included in the selling price and selling expenses. Often preplanning can take the sting out of paying too much.

■ Chapter 2 Review Questions

1. If the buyer assumes a mortgage, that amount must be included in the selling price.

   a. True

   b. False

2. Only the cash down payment is included in the selling price, not the assumed mortgages.

   a. True

   b. False

3. Prorated taxes and finance charges paid by the buyer may be included in "selling expenses."

   a. True

   b. False

4. Generally, adjusted basis is original cost plus improvements minus depreciation.

   a. True

   b. False

5. In many cases, the taxpayer would pay less taxes if the option were held for more than 12 months and sold rather than exercised.

   a. True

   b. False

6. Once the taxpayer rents out the home, depreciation allowances will decrease the property basis, whether "used" or not.

   a. True

   b. False

7. Sale price minus original cost equals gain or loss.

   a. True

   b. False

8. The buyer and seller can use two different selling prices on the same piece of property.

   a. True

   b. False

9. When property is received as a gift, the transfer must be reported by the recipient as a gift for income tax purposes.

   a. True

   b. False

10. Repair expenditures on investment property may be deducted against the rental income unless they substantially improve the property.

    a. True

    b. False

Exclusion Rule for Gain on Sale of Principal Residence

learning objectives

Upon completing this chapter, you will be able to:

- define principal residence;

- explain when the gain realized on the sale or exchange of a principal residence is free;

- identify the tax planning ideas that have been replaced (i.e., 24-month rollover and over-55 one-time exclusion);

- summarize the §121 requirements to exclude up to $250,000, or $500,000 if married filing jointly, from gross income; and

- explain what happens when one spouse qualifies and the other does not.

■ Key Terms

§121 qualification   MFJ (married filing jointly)   principal residence

■ Overview

Two provisions in the tax code have greatly assisted taxpayers over the years: the principal residence rollover provision (i.e., buy up within 24 months) and the exclusion rule (i.e., $125,000 of gain forgiven). However, these rules did not meet the needs of many people: the retiree or empty nester who sells the large family residence and purchases a substantially less expensive home, the divorcee who is now renting an apartment, or the homeowner who moves from a high-cost area to a low-cost area (from San Francisco to Casper, Wyoming).

Tax Tip! Always check with your tax advisor, as IRS regulations are frequently revised and/or interpreted by court decision.

Congress concluded that the reinvestment requirement of the rollover provision was an undesirable burden, and the $125,000 was not large enough. Therefore, effective for sales on or after May 7, 1997, Congress repealed both the §1034 rollover statute and the old §121 one-time over-55 exclusion rule and provided a new §121 relief provision applicable to principal residences (Taxpayers Relief Act of 1997, referred to as TRA97).

This chapter describes various tax consequences when selling a personal residence and provides specific examples of the requirements necessary for homeowners to use the new §121 exclusion of gain rule.

■ What Is the Definition of a Principal Residence?

Because this large exclusion of gain applies only to the taxpayer's "principal" residence and because the definition of principal residence is the area in which most of the tax problems and IRS controversies arise, it is important to the taxpayer to recognize the issues. Defining principal residence covers four major categories:

1. Types of qualified properties
2. Ownership requirements
3. Occupancy requirements
4. Residences used also for business

■ Where Is Your Principal Residence?

A taxpayer's principal residence is the land and the building where the taxpayer principally domiciles, based upon all the facts and circumstances in each case, including the good faith of the taxpayer. It may even be located in a foreign country [Rev. Rul. 54-611].

When multiple homes are owned, the principal residence may be where the taxpayer spends the "majority of time." In addition to the taxpayer's use of the property, relevant factors in determining a taxpayer's principal residence include but are not limited to:

- the taxpayer's place of employment;
- the principal place of abode of the taxpayer's family members;
- the address listed on the taxpayer's federal and state tax returns, driver's license, automobile registration, and voter registration card;
- the taxpayer's mailing address for bills and correspondence;
- the location of the taxpayer's banks; and
- the location of religious organizations and recreational clubs with which the taxpayer is affiliated [§1.121-1 (b)(2)(i) – (iv); also see Rev. Rul. 71-247].

Only One "Principal" Residence

One taxpayer cannot own two principal residences simultaneously, as principal is defined as "the most important" [*McDowell v. Comm.*, 40 TCM 301(1980)].

Each Spouse May Have a Separate "Principal" Residence

Each spouse would be able to separately exclude $250,000 as long as each satisfies all the qualification requirements. This allows spouses who both own homes to each exclude up to $250,000 in gain, just as if they were filing separately.

Property That May Qualify

A personal residence may be a single-family house, condominium, cooperative, mobile home, boat, houseboat, a house trailer, or motorhome [previous §1.1034-1(c)(3)(i)].

■ When Is the Gain FREE?

In general, the exclusion rule provides that up to $250,000 of gain ($500,000 if MFJ) realized on the sale or exchange of a principal residence is not taxable (not just deferred) if certain prerequisites are satisfied. This permanent exclusion is allowed each time a homeowner meets the eligibility requirements, but generally no more frequently than once every two years [§121].

The gain is free when the taxpayer can prove the following:

- The sales price of the home was $250,000 or under ($500,000 if married and filing a joint return [MFJ]);

  or

- The costs of improvements eliminate any taxable gain (i.e., above $250,000/ $500,000 MFJ);

  and

- The original cost of the home sold (generally done by making HUD Form 1 available to the IRS auditor);

  and

- That no more than one home has been reported in the previous two years from the sale date;

  and

- That no prior depreciation has been taken on the home after May 7, 1997.

■ What Tax Planning Requirements Are Obsolete?

1. There is no requirement to reinvest the sales proceeds into another home, i.e., taxpayers do not have to buy equal or up within 24 months.
2. The requirement that the taxpayer must be at least age 55 has been repealed.
3. Fixing-up expenses, including "conditions-of-sale" repairs, are no longer deductible anywhere.
4. The "moving at least 50 miles" requirement to avoid the once-every-two-years rule has been eliminated.
5. The nontaxable gain does not have to be "rolled over" into the new home.
6. Renting the home while trying to sell it generally will not cause tax problems.

This new exclusion eliminates most record-keeping requirements when home sellers absolutely know in the future they will not experience a home gain of more than $250,000 ($500,000 for married couples filing jointly). Starting for sales after May 6, 1997, the IRS will NOT receive notification of any home sale up to $250,000 ($500,000 MFJ) via Form 1099-S by the real estate closing agent (e.g., the title company, real estate broker, or mortgage company).

The home seller will have to provide the agent "assurances" that

- the home was a "principal residence," and
- there was no federally subsidized mortgage financing assistance, and
- the full gain is excludable from gross income (e.g., no depreciation recapture).

The IRS has the authority to increase the dollar amount in the future [§6045(e)(5)].

■ New Tax Planning Tips

Claim Your State of Residency with Care

Suppose you own and use two homes, one in California and one in Nevada, during a part of each year. Because Nevada has no state income taxes, you have been claiming Nevada as your state of residence by saying that you reside in your Nevada home the majority of each year. When you sell your California home, the gain is not excludable because it is not your principal personal residence. To exclude the California gain, you must use the California home as your principal residence at least two of five years. State tax returns should match that claim.

Contractors Can Qualify for Exclusion on "Spec House"

If you are a contractor or very handy with a hammer and nail, consider building a "spec house." When the house is completed, move into it as your principal residence for two plus years. If the house has been your principal residence for two of the past five years, when it is sold, you are entitled to exclude up to $250,000 of the gain ($500,000 on a married filing jointly return if otherwise qualified). This occupancy changes the gain from ordinary self-employment income to found money.

Exclusion Rule Is Optional, Not Mandatory

Taxpayer(s) may elect out of this rule and have the gain taxable [§121(f)].

Dolores marries Alfred on January 1. On May 15, they sell Alfred's old home for a $10,000 gain. On January 15 of the following year, they sell Dolores's home for a $500,000 MFJ gain.

It would be smarter for Alfred to elect to make his $10,000 gain taxable so that Dolores and Alfred can file jointly and use their combined $500,000 MFJ exclusion. If he uses the exclusion against the $10,000, he cannot again use the exclusion until two years later, and Dolores could exclude only $250,000.

Wealthy Homeowners May Be Forced To Report Gain

The amount in excess of the $250,000/$500,000 MFJ exclusion must be included as capital gain income, even if all of the sales proceeds are reinvested in a new residence. For these homeowners, the old repealed §1034 "rollover" provision had more benefits. (Taxpayers can do an "installment sale" for all gains over $250,000/$500,000 MFJ.)

Exchanging Personal Residences

Occasionally homeowners will exchange one personal residence for another personal residence (common in farm exchanges) instead of selling them. Exchanges of personal residences are not eligible for tax-free exchanges, and, therefore, the rules of this chapter apply both to sales and exchanges of homes.

■ What Are the §121 Qualification Requirements?

If the taxpayer meets both qualifications mentioned below, up to $250,000/ $500,000 MFJ of gain may be excluded from gross income [§121(b)(1) and (2)]:

1. **Own and occupy for two years:** The taxpayer must own and use the home as his or her principal residence for a total of two years during the five-year period ending on the date of the sale or exchange [§121(a)] *(with three notable exceptions, discussed later).*

and

2. **No more than once every two years:** During the two-year period ending on the date of sale, the taxpayer cannot report another sale or exchange to which §121 applies [§121(b)(3)].

Dating the Sale

The date of sale is generally the earlier of the date "a deed passes (the date of the delivery of the deed) or at the time possession and the burdens and benefits of ownership [from a practical standpoint] are transferred to the buyer" [Rev. Rul. 69-93].

Rashida sells her principal residence for $330,000. She had purchased the home 20 years earlier for $40,000 and had added a $25,000 recreation room to it. She pays commissions and other closing costs of $30,000. Her total gain is nontaxable if she uses the $250,000 exclusion rule (see Figure 3.1).

$500,000 Exclusion When Four Requirements Are Met

The $250,000 exclusion doubles to $500,000 MFJ if the following four requirements are met:

1. A husband and wife make a joint return for the taxable year of the sale or exchange of the property; and
2. Either spouse owns the property for two of the last five years; and
3. Both spouses use the property as their principal residence for two of the last five years; and
4. Neither spouse is ineligible because more than one sale or exchange has been used during the previous two years [§121(b)(2)].

Figure 3.1 | Gain or Loss Calculation

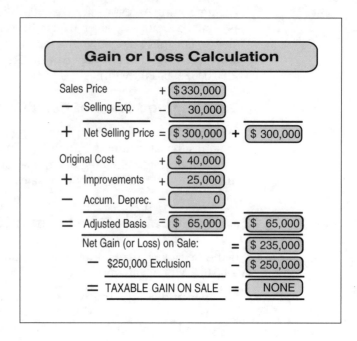

If the stated requirements are NOT met, a married couple will, at a minimum, be eligible for the $250,000 exclusion if either spouse meets all the requirements.

The two-year requirement does not prevent a husband and wife from filing a joint return for each excluding up to $250,000 of gain from the sale of each spouse's principal residence, provided that each spouse would be permitted to exclude up to $250,000 of gain if they filed separate returns.

This would seem to allow a couple to have two principal residences if they are not living together but are still filing jointly.

■ What Happens if One Spouse Qualifies and the Other Does Not Qualify?

If a husband and wife make a joint return for the taxable year of the sale or exchange of the principal residence, the $250,000 exclusion rule and the proration of gain rule apply if either spouse meets the ownership and use requirements [§121(d)(1)]. Similarly, if a single taxpayer who is otherwise eligible for an exclusion marries someone who has used the exclusion within the two years prior to the marriage, the newly married taxpayer is allowed a maximum exclusion of $250,000.

Once both spouses satisfy the eligibility rules, however, and two years have passed since the last exclusion was allowed to either of them, the taxpayers may exclude $500,000 MFJ of gain on their joint return.

The determination of whether an individual is married shall be determined by the election to make a joint return, not as of the date of the sale or exchange [§1.6013-1(a)].

Owning a Home with a "Significant Other"

If two unmarried individuals jointly own and use one principal residence, the $250,000 exclusion provisions should apply independently to each on a sale of the residence. The home is treated like a duplex owned by a joint venture partnership.

Determining at Least Two of the Last Five Years

During the five-year period ending on the date of the sale or exchange, the taxpayer must have owned and used the property as a principal residence for periods aggregating two years or more. This two-year ownership and use requirement may be satisfied by establishing ownership and use for either 24 full months or 730 days (365 days x 2) during the 60-month time period prior to sale [§121(a); §1.121-1(c)(1)].

Therefore, the ownership and use requirement can be met in two years; if a homeowner owns and uses the same home for two years, he or she has automatically met the "two-of-the-last-five-years requirement."

Ownership and Use Need NOT Be Simultaneous

Satisfaction of both conditions must occur within the five-year period ending on the date of the sale or exchange. In other words, a tenant who purchases the home can count the time as a tenant as part of the use requirement. Also, a homeowner can rent out his or her home and still count that time toward the ownership requirements [Rev. Rul. 80-172].

Occasional Absences

Short, temporary absences, such as vacations or other seasonal absences, even when accompanied by rental of the residence, are counted as periods of use [previous §1.121-1(c)]. A one-year sabbatical leave, however, is not considered a short, temporary absence [previous §1.121-1(d) (Example 5)].

Rentals Are NOT Primary Residences

A homeowner who converts a principal residence into a rental may be faced with a realized and taxable gain in a future sale. Once the personal residence has been rented for more than three of the last five years, the $250,000/$500,000 MFJ exclusion rule is not usable because the property is no longer deemed a principal residence. The taxpayer would be required to reoccupy the property as a principal residence for two of the last five years before the sale to reestablish the principal-residence status.

There is no exclusion for rentals! Owners of rentals may use the 1031 tax-free (like-kind) exchange rules to defer gain. **Note:** There are no definitive court cases addressing this question. Generally, renting the property for three years or more will make the property eligible for an exchange.

Physically or Mentally Incapacitated

The two-of-the-last-five-years rule was liberalized to include a taxpayer who during the five-year period (1) owns and uses the residence for at least one year (not two years) and (2) becomes physically or mentally incapable of self-care during the five years, thereafter residing in a state-licensed facility (including a nursing home) [§121(d)(6)].

On January 1 Edith purchased and moved into her new personal residence. On July 31 of the following year, she moved into the Powder River County Memorial Nursing Home but didn't sell the house until six months after moving into the nursing home. Because Edith owned and occupied the principal residence for 1 1/2 years (e.g., at least one year), plus she resided in the nursing home for six more months (i.e., thus meeting the two-year ownership rule), she is entitled to use the $250,000/$500,000 MFJ.

Exclusion Available Only Once Every Two Years

The $250,000/$500,000 MFJ exclusion rule does not apply if there are any other exclusion sales or exchanges used by the taxpayer during the two-year period ending on the date of sale or exchange [§121(b)(3)(A)].

■ What if a Homeowner Can't Meet the Two-Year Rule?

Some (or all) of the generally taxable gain may be tax free, even if the taxpayer cannot meet the two-of-last-five-years-rule ownership test, or the use test, or has used this exclusion rule within the last two years if the primary reason is one of the following:

- Change in place of employment
- Health problems
- Other unforeseen circumstances, as provided in IRS regulations [§121(c)(2)]

Sale or Exchange by Reason of Change in Place of Employment

If the taxpayer's primary reason for the sale or exchange is a change in the location of the employment of a qualified individual, the reduced exclusion rule is available to the homeowner [TR §1.121-3T(c)(1)]. A *qualified individual* includes the taxpayer, the taxpayer's spouse, a co-owner of the residence, or a member of the taxpayer's household [TR §1.121-3(f)(1-4)].

The following are possible examples:

- Being transferred by employer 12 months after purchasing a new home would qualify.
- A change in the availability of public transportation because of employment location may be a primary reason for sale.
- A promotion to a managerial position may require a higher level of "entertainment" at home, necessitating a new home.

Relief is available to new employees, transfers, and even the self-employed: Employment means the commencement of employment with a new employer, the continuation of employment with the same employer, or the commencement of self-employment.

The 50-mile safe harbor rule: A home sale will be considered related to a change in employment (i.e., a safe harbor) if one of the above mentioned qualified person's new place of work is at least 50 miles farther from the old home than the old workplace was from that home. If the individual was unemployed, the distance between the new place of employment and the residence sold or exchanged must be at least 50 miles. The safe harbor applies only if the change in place of employment occurs during the period of the taxpayer's ownership and use of the property as the taxpayer's principal residence [TR §1.121-3T(c)(2)].

The facts and circumstances test: If a sale or exchange does not satisfy the 50-mile safe harbor, a taxpayer may still qualify for the reduced maximum exclusion if the facts and circumstances indicate that a change in place of employment is the primary reason for the sale or exchange.

Sale or Exchange by Reason of Health

If the *primary reason* a principal residence is sold is related to a disease, illness, or injury of a *qualified individual* (the taxpayer, the taxpayer's spouse, a co-owner of the residence, a person whose principal place of abode is in the same household as the taxpayer, or other close family members of these individuals, such as children, parents, siblings, aunts, uncles, and in-laws [see §152(a)(1) through (8)], even when not living in the same household), the sale proceeds are eligible for the reduced maximum exclusion rule [TR §1.121-3T(d)(1)].

In this case, *qualifying taxpayers* could include:

- an injured taxpayer who moves in with a daughter [TR §1.121-3T(d)(3), Ex 1];
- a healthy taxpayer who moves closer to an ill parent [TR §1.121-3T(d)(3), Ex 2];
- taxpayers who move so that their child can be closer to a particular hospital [TR §1.121-3T(d)(3), Ex 3];
- an asthmatic taxpayer who moves from Michigan to Arizona [TR §1.121-3T(d)(3), Ex 4];

Physician safe harbor rule: A safe harbor is established if a licensed physician [as defined in §213(d)(4)] recommends a change of residence for the previously described "reasons of health." A sale or exchange that is merely beneficial to the general health or well-being of the individual is *not* a sale or exchange by reasons of health [TR §1.121-3T(d)(1) & (2)].

Chuck and Helen live in Michigan, and Chuck has been told by his physician that it is a good idea to get more exercise, but he does not have a specific disease that could be treated or mitigated by exercise. When they move to Florida, they cannot claim a reduced maximum exclusion. The sale is merely beneficial to Chuck's general well-being, and not for "reasons of health." [TR §1.121-3T(d)(3), Ex. 5].

Jeff, a taxpayer in Minnesota, is told by his physician that life in a warm, dry climate would mitigate his asthma symptoms. When Jeff sells his house to move to Arizona, he is entitled to claim a reduced maximum exclusion [TR §1.121-3T(d)(3), Ex.4].

Sale or Exchange by Reason of Unforeseen Circumstances

A sale or exchange is by reason of "unforeseen circumstances" if the primary reason for the sale is the occurrence of an event that the taxpayer did not anticipate before purchasing an occupying residence [TR §1.121-3T(e)(1)].

Definition of *qualified individual:* Sales proceeds or insurance awards are eligible for the reduced maximum exclusion if a principal residence is required to be sold because one of the four following individuals—the taxpayer, the taxpayer's spouse, a co-owner of the residence, or a person whose principal place of abode is in the same household as the taxpayer—experiences an unforeseen circumstance that the homeowner did not anticipate before purchasing and occupying the residence [TR §1.121-3T(f)].

Safe harbors relating to the physical structure include:

1. condemnation or other involuntary conversions: the home was condemned for public use (e.g., condemned for public highway use) or stolen (e.g., theft of a motor home);
2. damage to the home by natural or man-made disaster: the home was destroyed by a natural disaster (e.g., fire, earthquake, or hurricane) or a man-made disaster (e.g., act-of-war or terrorism) [TR §1.121-3T(e)(3), Ex. 1; also see IRS Notice 2002-60].

Other unforeseen circumstances qualifying as safe harbors include:

1. death [TR §1.121-3T(e)(2)];
2. cessation of employment, making the individual eligible for unemployment compensation [TR §1.121-3T(e)(2)];
3. change in job creating inability to pay mortgage or household expenses: a change in employment (e.g., demotion or layoff) or self-employment status that results in the taxpayer's inability to pay housing costs and reasonable basic living expenses for the taxpayer's household [TR §1.121-3T(e)(3), Ex. 2];
4. divorce or legal separation: divorce or legal separation under a decree of divorce or separate maintenance [TR §1.121-3T(e)(2)]; and
5. multiple births from the same pregnancy, e.g., the birth of twins or triplets, making a recently purchased two-bedroom home too small [TR §1.121-3T(e)(3), Ex. 3; TR §1.121-3T(e)(1)-(3)].

A taxpayer who does not qualify for one of the above safe harbors may still demonstrate that the primary reason for the sale or exchange is unforeseen circumstances, under a *facts and circumstances test*, which could include such circumstances as:

1. a radical increase in association dues (e.g., a doubling of condo dues) unanticipated at a time of purchase [TR §1.121-3T(e)(3), Ex. 4], or
2. engagement breakup [TR §1.121-3T(e)(3), Ex. 6].

In addition, the IRS may designate other events or situations as unforeseen circumstances in published guidance of general applicability or in a ruling directed to a specific taxpayer.

Prorating the Excludable Gain

If neither of the two-year requirements are met, but the taxpayer meets one of the three preceding criteria, then a portion of the otherwise taxable gain may be excluded on a prorated basis. The exclusion factor (i.e., proration percentage) is computed by dividing the "use period" or the period "between the two sales dates" (whichever is less) by 730 days (i.e., 2 years). The amount of excludable gain allowed is prorated by multiplying the maximum allowable exclusion (limited to $250,000 or $500,000 MFJ) by the exclusion factor (proration percentage).

Days in Use or Between Sales

730 (number of days in 2 years)

- Total Gain × Exclusion % = Excludable Gain
- This is capped at $250,000 or $500,000 MFJ; check with a tax professional.

> *B.J. used her $250,000 exclusion on the sale of her principal residence, which closed on July 18 and then purchased a new principal residence in the same month on July 29. Due to "unforeseen circumstances" she had to sell her principal residence on July 28 of the following year for a $70,000 gain after owning it for only one year. She is permitted to exclude the entire gain, as the gain didn't exceed the maximum 50% exclusion (365 ÷ 730 = 50%) of $125,000 ($250,000 × 50% = $125,000 permitted exclusion).*

Calculation of partial exclusion for 12-month ownership; 24 months is the required ownership period for full exclusion; $70,000 capital gain:

$$\frac{12}{24} \times \$250,000 = \$125,000$$

Because $70,000 is less than $125,000, no tax is due.

Any capital gain over $125,000 would be taxable.

> *Rene sells her home exactly one year after purchasing it to take a new job in another city. She realizes a $20,000 gain on the sale. She is allowed to exclude $125,000 (50% of $250,000).*

The exclusion calculation works to the detriment of people who realize very large gains, as shown in the following case:

> *For health reasons, the Maxwells are forced to sell their mansion after living there only 18 months. They realize a gain of $800,000 on the sale and are entitled to exclude $375,000 for tax purposes (75% of $500,000).*

■ What Happens after Death or Divorce?

"Tacking" of a Deceased Spouse's Ownership and Use Allowed

When a surviving spouse sells the jointly used principal residence in a year following death, the surviving spouse must now file as a single taxpayer, but the surviving spouse's ownership and use period includes the deceased spouse's ownership period before the death [§121(d)(2)].

Spousal Exclusion Expires the Next Year

If one spouse dies, and the home is sold in the year of the deceased spouse's death, the surviving spouse can file as married filing jointly, thus retaining the $500,000 MFJ exclusion. If the home is sold in a subsequent year, the spouse is usually required to file as single, with only the $250,000 exclusion available.

This may not be a severe problem, because under current estate taxation, the decedent's share of the principal residence usually experiences a "stepped-up" basis, thereby eliminating one-half the gain [§1014]. Also, in a community-property state, the entire gain may be stepped up, depending on how title is held. Only survivors with a gain exceeding $500,000 MFJ might need tax planning advice in this regard.

> **Purchase but Not Occupy Is Not Sufficient:** If a homeowner purchases a house but does not significantly use the residence, and instead occupies a rental apartment, the rental apartment becomes the homeowner's new principal residence.
>
> This occupancy requirement is not satisfied by simply moving in furniture without personally occupying [*John F. Bayley*, 35 TC 288 (1960); *Anne Franklin Society*, 33 TC 614 (1958)], nor by using the residence on weekends or vacations (*William C. Stolk*, 40 TC 345 (1963)], nor by allowing a child of the taxpayer to occupy the property [Rev. Rul. 69-143, 1969-2 CB 163].

Don and Janice marry on January 1. At that time, Janice moves into Don's residence, which he had owned and used for more than five years. Don dies one year later, on January 1, and Janice inherits the property. She continues to use the property as her personal residence for another eight months, until August 31, at which time she sells it (less than two years after moving in).

She may still make a $500,000 MFJ exclusion because, during the five-year period ending on the date of the sale (August 31), Don had previously satisfied the two-year ownership and use requirements. As Don's surviving spouse, Janice can "tack" his ownership and use onto hers. If she had waited until two years after her marriage she would not need to "tack" Don's time, but she would qualify for only a $250,000 single exclusion.

Tacking of Ownership in Divorce

When property is transferred between spouses during marriage or subsequent to divorce, no gain or loss is recognized, and the transfer is treated similarly to a gift [§1014]. The recipients period of use of such property shall include the period the transferor owned the property [§121(d)(3)(A)].

Elizabeth marries and moves into Larry's long-time (more than five years) home on January 1. One month later they divorce and Elizabeth receives the home as part of her divorce settlement, which she immediately sells for $250,000 cash. Elizabeth's ownership period is deemed five years, not one month.

Tacking of a divorced spouse's previous "use" is not mentioned in the new exclusion rule, and thus it seems not to be permitted. In the above example, because Elizabeth is in possession of the residence at time of sale she would probably have to establish her own use period.

Tacking of Use in Divorce Allowed in One Situation

It is fairly common for divorce court to order the family home sold and the proceeds split between former spouses. It may also allow the parent granted custody of the children to be given use of the home rent-free until sale.

Prior to the 1997 tax code revisions, the IRS successfully made the argument that when the custodial parent's use period exceeds a "reasonable time" (i.e., two years), the noncustodial parent was not "using" that home as his or her principal residence at the time of sale. Thus, they taxed the noncustodial parent's gain [*D. D. Bowers*, TC Memo 1996-333; *C. B. Perry*, CA-9, 96-2 USTC, ¶50, 405].

The blatant unfairness of the above situation has now been corrected. Under the new rules, an individual shall be treated as using property as a principal residence during any period of ownership while such individual's spouse or former spouse is granted use of the property under a divorce or separation instrument [§121(d)(3)(B)].

■ Does Renting the Home or Using It for Business Affect the Exclusion?

Rentals Still Qualify if Residence for Two of Five Years

As long as the home is owned and used as a primary residence two out of the five years prior to the sale date, it retains its personal residence character and does not become a taxable rental property [§121(a)].

When a personal residence is listed for sale during a "down" or "slow" market, it is common to rent the house until it is sold. Under prior law, care was needed to ensure that the property retained its personal residence character and did not convert to a rental (which wasn't eligible for either the prior rollover provision or exclusion rule).

The new §121 provides a definition of time, i.e., the home can be rented three out of five years before it converts into a rental and thus becomes ineligible for the $250,000/$500,000 MFJ exclusion.

The preceding "tax loophole" allows homeowners to rent their home for up to three years while striving to sell it. Many taxpayers will be tempted to rent their residence and wait for someone to offer their asking price instead of accepting a lower counteroffer. Also, there is no requirement to keep the property listed during the rental period, as was required under prior law [*Clapham v. Comm.* 63TC 505 (1975)].

Home Can Be Depreciated While Rented

In *Bolaris v. Comm.*, [81 TC 840 (1983); 776 F2d 1428 (9th Cir 1985)], the Tax Court held as proper the taxpayer's deduction of rental expenses and "residential" depreciation. The court held that a residence that qualifies for the principal residence provisions may also qualify as property held for the production of income and, therefore, allowed *Bolaris* to not only take depreciation but also to defer the ensuing (prior law) gain [see also *Grant v. Comm.*, 84 TC 809 (1985)].

Any gain attributable to depreciation taken after May 6, 1997, with respect to the prior rental or business use of the principal residence must be recognized in the year of the sale (but, interestingly, not an exchange) [§121(d)(6); §1.121-1(d)(1)].

If the taxpayer does not take the allowable depreciation on a home office, the adjusted basis of the property must still be reduced by the allowable depreciation. This is because the amount recaptured is presumed to be the greater of the allowed (taken) and the allowable depreciation. But the IRS has taken the sting out of the "allowed or allowable" rule by permitting the investor to take the previously unreported depreciation all in the year of the sale [Rev. Proc. 2004-11].

Home Used for Both Personal and Business Purposes on Sale Date

No allocation of gain is required if both the residential and nonresidential portions of the property are within the same dwelling unit. The fact that a residence is rented or is used partially for business (i.e., a home office) at the time of the sale does not disqualify the gain attributable to the business use, other than depreciation recapture, from the $250,000/$500,000 exclusion. But the §121 exclusion will not apply to the gain allocable to any portion of property sold or exchanged with respect to which a taxpayer does not satisfy the use requirement of the nonresidential portion is separate from the dwelling unit [§1.121-1(e)(1)]. The final regulations provide that the term *dwelling unit* has the same meaning as in §280A(f)(1) but does not include appurtenant structures or other property [§1.121-1(e)(2)].

Joan sells her personal residence, which contains her deductible office-in-home, for a $100,000 gain. She estimates that the office occupies 10% of her home. She can exclude the entire $100,000 gain other than any depreciation recapture. The $10,000 gain associated with the office-in-home is not taxable.

Depreciation recapture still required on office-in-home! But §121 does not apply to the gain to the extent of any post-May 6, 1997, depreciation adjustments [§121-1(e)(1)]. If the depreciation for periods after May 6, 1997, attributable to the nonresidential portion of the property exceeds the gain allocable to the nonresidential portion of the property, the excess will not reduce the §121 exclusion applicable to gain allocable to the residential property. The taxpayer must use the same method to allocate the basis and the amount realized between the business and residential portions of the property as the taxpayer used to allocate the basis for purposes of depreciation, if applicable [§121-1(e)(3)].

Loss on Sale of Residence Not Deductible

Even though the Internal Revenue Code requires immediate recognition of all gain on the sale or exchange of property, including a personal residence that is not excluded, any loss on the sale is nondeductible. The IRS considers the loss "personal, living, or family" expense [§1001(c); §262; §1.262-1(b)(4); §1.165-9(a)].

Converting Home into Rental May Make Loss Deductible

Theoretically it is possible to convert a personal residence into a business use prior to the sale date and thereby convert the otherwise nondeductible loss into a deductible one. However, it is difficult to do [§165(c)(1) and (2)], and it is unclear what length of time must elapse before the personal residence becomes a rental for tax purposes.

One argument in the taxpayer's favor is that how a residence is being used at the date of sale is of major importance in determining whether property is business or personal [*U.S. v. Winthrop*, (5 Cir. 1969)]. Therefore, the taxpayer must prove that the property was a rental when sold, and that the conversion was not done for tax purposes only [*William C. Horrmann*, 17 TC 903 (1951)].

Loss Prior to Conversion Not Deductible

The adjusted basis for determining a loss for property converted from personal use is the smaller of either the fair market value or adjusted basis of the property at the time of conversion. Therefore, any loss created prior to the conversion is not deductible either at the time of conversion or at the time of sale [§1.165-9(b)(2)].

■ How Much Land Can Be Sold with the Personal Residence?

Gain on land considered part of a personal residence can be excluded, but gain on land considered investment property, held for appreciation, or business property held for profit, is taxable and may not use the exclusion provisions. A sale of vacant land that does not include a dwelling unit does not qualify as a sale of a taxpayer's residence [§1.121-1(b)(3); Rev. Rul. 56-240; Rev. Rul. 83-50; *O'Barr v. Commissioner*, 44 T.C. 501 (1965); *Roy v. Commissioner*, T.C. Memo. 1995-23; *Hale v. Commisioner*, T.C. Memo. 1982-527]. However, if

- the vacant land is adjacent to land containing the principal residence;
- the vacant land was owned and used as part of the taxpayer's principal residence;
- the sale or exchange of the dwelling unit occurs within two years before or after the sale or exchange of the vacant land; and
- the sale or exchange of the vacant land satisfies all other §121 requirements, then the sale of the vacant land and the sale of the principal residence are treated as one sale eligible for the §121 exclusion [§1.121-1(b)(3)(i)(A-D); see also *Bogley v. Commissioner*, 263 F.2d 746 (4th Cir. 1959); Rev. Rul. 76-541]. Only one maximum limitation amount of $250,000 ($500,000 MFJ) applies to the combined sales or exchanges of the vacant land and dwelling unit [§1.121-1(b)(3)(ii)].

In 1998, Chad buys a house and one acre that serves as his principal residence. In 1999, he buys 29 acres adjacent to his house and uses the vacant land as part of his principal residence. This year Chad sells the house and one acre and the 29 acres to two separate transactions. He sells the house and one acre at a loss of $25,000. Chad realizes a $270,000 gain from the sale of the 29 acres and may exclude the $245,000 gain from the two sales [§1.121 – 1(b)(4), Ex.4].

Sandy buys a home with ten acres of land as her primary residence in 1991. In May 2005 she sells eight acres of the land for a gain of $110,000. She does not sell the house before the due date for filing her 2005 return, therefore Sandy is not eligible to exclude the gain. In March 2007 she sells the house and the remaining two acres, realizing a gain of $180,000 from the sale of the house. Sandy may exclude the $180,000. Also, because the sale of the eight acres occurred within two years from the date of the sale of the house, the sale of the eight acres is treated as a sale of the taxpayer's principal residence [§1.121-1(b)(3)]. Sandy may file an amended return for 2005 to claim an exclusion for $70,000 ($250,000 - $180,000 gain previously excluded) of the $110,000 gain from the sale of the eight acres [§1.121 –1(b)(4), Ex.3].

The "one-acre" rule! Unofficially, the IRS, in farm communities, considers one acre to be associated with the home unless the taxpayer proves that more than one acre is not used for income-producing purposes.

■ Conclusion

For many taxpayers, reporting gain on the sale of a primary residence has become much simpler. For married couples who sell their home for less than $500,000, none of the gain is taxable as long as they have not excluded another home gain within two years and took no depreciation after May 7, 1997 (i.e., they did not deduct an office-in-home) or rented out their primary residence after May 7, 1997.

However, married taxpayers will now have to pay taxes on capital gains in excess of $500,000 on the sale of their primary residence, even if they purchase a more expensive home within two years. This is a major change from prior tax law.

The recent changes will encourage many baby boomers to consider selling their large home and to "buy-down" to a smaller, less expensive home.

■ Chapter 3 Review Questions

1. A property owner who sells his primary residence must purchase another home at the same or higher price to avoid paying capital gains tax.

    a. True

    b. False

2. To benefit from the new rules, homeowners must own and occupy their home for at least two of the five years prior to sale or exchange.

    a. True

    b. False

3. A tenant who subsequently purchases a property can count the time when renting it as part of the use requirement.

    a. True

    b. False

4. A taxpayer may claim two primary residences.

    a. True

    b. False

5. If a taxpayer does not live in his home for the prescribed period (two years), he may still exclude, if qualified, a portion of the gain from taxes.

    a. True

    b. False

6. If a taxpayer is prevented from occupying her new home for the full two years because of "unforeseen circumstances," she may retain a portion of the exclusion.

    a. True

    b. False

7. In a divorce, the parent who has moved out of the home may still claim it as a principal residence for tax purposes in certain circumstances.

    a. True

    b. False

8. Homeowners may not rent their home for more than six months while it is offered for sale, or they will forfeit the $500,000 MFJ exclusion.

    a. True

    b. False

9. When a principal residence is sold for a loss, the taxpayer can deduct the loss from that year's taxable income.

    a. True

    b. False

10. In rural areas the IRS normally considers one acre of land to be associated with the home.

    a. True

    b. False

chapter four

Applying the Passive Loss Rules to Real Estate Professionals

learning objectives

Upon completing this chapter, you will be able to:

- explain RREAs (rental real estate activities);
- summarize requirements for material participation in rental activities;
- discuss the three common tests to define material participation for real estate investors; and
- list at least three types of taxpayers who will benefit from the 50% participation and 750-hour requirements.

Key Terms

material participation | passive participation | RREAs

Overview

Prior to the Tax Reform Act of 1986 (TRA 86), no limitations were placed on the ability of a taxpayer to use deductions, losses, or credits from one business or investment to offset the profits of another business or investment. This allowed the opportunity for taxpayers to offset, or "shelter," the income from one source with deductions and credits from another source.

Pre-1986 Tax Shelter

Brad, an attorney, receives a $150,000 salary. He is married, has no children, and has itemized deductions of $10,000. His limited partnership investments in real estate create a $140,000 loss. Brad owes no taxes, as his real estate loss is fully *deductible against his salary income. Without the real estate deduction, Brad would have approximately $32,300 tax liability.*

By 1986, Congress determined that the average taxpayer was losing faith in the federal income tax system in part because of abusive tax shelters. The congressional solution to limiting tax shelters without eliminating tax preferences to certain businesses and activities (such as tax benefits given to low-income housing, rehabilitation of older buildings, and farming) is to benefit and provide incentives only to taxpayers either materially or actively involved in their businesses.

Closing the Loopholes

Since 1987, taxpayers must "materially participate" in the business to be eligible for most tax incentives. Tax preference benefits are directed primarily to taxpayers with a substantial and bona fide involvement in the activities to which the preferences relate. Therefore, even though Congress wants to continue giving tax preferences, it does not want those preferences used against unrelated income.

Brad, in the previous example, no longer can deduct the real estate loss against his salary income, and his tax refund is reduced by approximately $32,300.

■ The §469 Passive Activity Loss Rules (PAL Rules)

Congress simply states that losses (and credits) from passive trade or business activities, to the extent they exceed income from all such passive activities generally, may not be deducted against other income such as salaries and wages or interest and dividends.

Exception to the Rule

The one major exception is the ability of middle-income taxpayers to deduct up to $25,000 of rental losses from "actively managed" real estate [§469(a)].

Ellie is a real estate agent with a commission income of $40,000. She is married with no children and has itemized deductions of $8,000. She purchases a certified historic apartment house for $5,000, assumes an underlying mortgage, and rehabilitates the property. At the end of the year, she receives a rental income schedule from her accountant reporting a $15,000 rental loss and $500 of rehabilitation tax credit. The $25,000 relief provision allows Ellie to offset her salary and commission income with the real estate losses and credits if she actively participates in the management of the apartment house.

Deduct Passive Losses from Passive Income

With limited exceptions, the PAL rules continue to allow losses and credits from one passive activity to be applied against income for the taxable year from another passive activity. As a result, taxpayers must divide their income into three separate "buckets":

1. **Active:** Salary, wages, personal services, and income from businesses (material participation)

2. **Passive:** Discussed in this chapter
3. **Portfolio:** Interest, dividends, royalties, annuities, and investment income

---

Dan is an accountant with a W-2 salary income of $40,000. He is married, has no children, and claims $8,000 of itemized deductions. He invests $5,000, plus recourse notes, in a real estate limited partnership tax shelter at the suggestion of his real estate broker.

At the end of the year, he receives a K-1 partnership tax schedule from the real estate company reporting that a $15,000 operating loss is allocated to him. Because of the "passive-limitation rule," the total $15,000 loss is nondeductible. He cannot use the $25,000 relief provision inasmuch as he is a limited partner who cannot "actively participate."

The attempt by Congress to halt investments in tax shelters while encouraging savings and investments in active businesses has had a significant impact on real estate investments.

One of the most unfair tax provisions passed in 1986 was the general rule that all real estate rental activities must be treated passively, no matter what the owner's level of participation [§469(c)(2)].

Example (Prior to the relief provision):

Marilyn, a full-time real estate agent making $160,000 in commissions each year, purchased an apartment complex in 1991 throwing off a $40,000 loss. From 1991 to 1993, none of this $40,000 loss was deductible. The $25,000 relief provision was not available to Marilyn as she makes more than $150,000 in modified income. She is carrying forward $120,000 of rental losses deductible against future rental income or deductible when the property is sold.

Relief Provision (RREAs)

Beginning January 1, 1994, a taxpayer's rental real estate activities (RREAs) in which he or she materially participates are not subject to limitation under the passive loss rule if the taxpayer meets eligibility requirements relating to real property trades or businesses in which the taxpayer performs services.

Real estate investors who qualify are now permitted to deduct their rental real estate losses from their current commissions, wages, interest, and dividends [§469(c)(7)].

General Rule

The only RREAs that qualify for this exceptional relief provision are real property rentals in which the qualified taxpayer materially participates in the management and operation of the RREAs.

This information will not help taxpayers who are not materially participating in their real estate investments.

Material Participation

Material participation in a trade or business activity is participation on a "regular, continuous, and substantial" basis. The regulations separately define the words "participation" and "material" [§469(h)(1)].

Material

There are seven tests, although most real estate investors meet the "materially" participating rule by one or more of the first three tests:

1. Managing and operating the rental real estate activity for more than 500 hours during the year.

or

2. Doing substantially all the work required to manage and operate the rental real estate during the year (probably more than 70% of the total business hours are performed by the landlord).

or

3. Working more than 100 hours during the year with no one (including non-owner employees and independent property managers) participating more than the landlord [Reg. §1.469-5T (a)(1)-(3)].

   However, an owner can "tack" a spouse's time for calculating the tests mentioned above (e.g., an owner/investor performing 51 hours could add a spouse's time of 50 hours to exceed the 100-hour requirement) [Reg. §1.469-5T(f)(3)].

or

4. Working 500 hours in all the multiple small businesses owned. This is for the taxpayer who has his or her fingers in many pies.

or

5. Materially participating for five of the last ten years. The years do not have to be consecutive, and only the 500-hour rule (test 1 above) may be used [Reg. §1.469-5(j)].

or

6. Materially participating in any three previous years in a "personal service activity." These could be in the field of health, law, engineering, architecture, etc. [§1.448T(e)(4)] or any other trade or business in which capital is not a material income-producing factor [Reg. §1.469-5T(a)(6); also §1.469-5T(d)].

or

7. "Facts-and-Circumstances" test. A taxpayer who does not satisfy any of the previous six tests may try to convince the IRS that he or she is materially participating (or not materially participating if he or she wants the income determined passive) based on all the facts and circumstances. One would have to prove participation on a "regular, continuous, and substantial basis."

Participation

An individual is said to "participate" when doing any work in any capacity, management or operations, in connection with an activity in which the individual owns an interest (directly or indirectly other than through a C corporation). This is not available if the owner does **only** the following:

■ Studies and reviews financial statements or monitors the finances or operations in a nonmanagerial capacity (e.g., acting as or being a limited partner).

or

■ The work is not "customarily performed" by owners, and one of the principal purposes of such work is avoiding the passive loss rules [§1.469-5T(f)(1)] (e.g., Donald Trump acting as a gift wrapper at Trump Tower).

Proving Participation

The burden of proof is on the taxpayer to prove he or she did (or did not) work the required hours a year, and taxpayers will find the courts difficult to convince without good records [*Goshorn v. Comm.*, 66 TCM 1499, TC Memo 1993-578; *Toups v. Comm.*, 66 TCM 1993-359].

Contemporaneous daily time reports, logs, or similar documents are not required if the extent of such participation may be established by other reasonable means.

Reasonable means can include, but are not limited to, the identification of services performed over a period of time and the approximate number of hours spent performing such services during such period, based on appointment books, calendars, or narrative summaries [§1.469-5T(f)(4)].

Aggregation of Rental Real Estate

Each interest of the taxpayer in rental real estate is to be considered as a separate activity, but a taxpayer may elect to treat all interests in real estate, including real estate held through passthrough entities, as one activity [§469(c)(7)(A)].

The above aggregation option permits the investor to meet the material participation test after cumulatively materially participating (e.g., spending 100 hours or 500 hours) in each activity, probably an impossible task for investors owning more than four rentals.

Properly Make Election

To make the election, the taxpayer files a statement with his or her original income tax return. This statement must contain a declaration that the taxpayer is a qualifying taxpayer for the taxable year and is making the election pursuant to section 469(c)(7)(A). The election to treat all interest in rental real estate as a single rental real estate activity is binding for all future years unless there is a material change in a taxpayer's facts and circumstances [Prop Reg. §1.469-9(g)].

Real Estate Owned by Passthrough Entities

If the taxpayer owns a 50% or greater interest in the capital, income, gain, loss, deduction, or credit of a passthrough at any time during a taxable year, each interest in rental real estate held by the passthrough entity will be treated as a separate interest in rental real estate, regardless of the passthrough entity's grouping of activities. However, the taxpayer may elect to treat it as a single rental real estate activity [Prop. Reg. §1.469-9(g)].

Applying the Passive Loss Rules to Vacation Condominiums

Property is not a rental, and instead is treated as a trade or business, if the average tenant use is seven days or less. Most tenant use of vacation homes averages less than seven days, which therefore makes tenants *ineligible* for the $25,000 relief provisions and requires that the owner meet the material participation tests before being eligible to exempt the loss from the passive loss limitation rules!

An individual participating in an activity for more than 100 hours during the taxable year is materially participating as long as the individual's participation in the activity for the taxable year is not less than the participation in the activity of any other individual (including nonowner employees) for such year.

Additionally, an individual participating in the activity for more than 500 hours during the taxable year is materially participating in that activity.

Taxpayer Loses on Vacation Home Deduction.   In a case involving the short-term rental of a vacation property, a couple was denied the ability to take a net loss on their tax return. In this instance, the couple used the management company that maintained the building to handle the reservations. A front desk staff, along with housekeeping department, was involved with the rentals as well. The couple visited the unit occasionally, attending owners' meetings and making repairs. But the couple did not "materially participate" in operating the property because they did *not* put in at least 100 hours, and *more than any other party* involved with the property. As an alternative, they could have participated at least 500 hours. However, there was no way that this would have been possible, given the distance of the property from their home. Because they failed to meet either of the tests, their deductions were limited to the total of the rental income they received. (*Barry H. Scheiner*, TC Memo 1996-554; J.O. *Patterson v. Comm.* TCS 2002-57.)

A Winning Arrangement for Vacation Home Deduction.   In another instance, a couple had a special arrangement with the management firm that operated the building in which the condo was located. Supposedly, while the company took care of all of the cleaning of the unit and supplied the front desk staff, the couple made all of the arrangements for advertising their place and actually renting it out. They estimated that this work involved about 200 hours each year. The tax court accepted their claim that they spent more time on their unit than the management company and therefore met the 100-hour test. *Key to the court's decision was the rejection of the IRS's contention that the time that the front desk was open should count as time for the management firm* [G. Pohoski, TC Memo 1998-17].

Previously Suspended Rental Losses

Although current losses can be deducted against other current active income, it is not as easy to "trigger" the prior rental losses not previously deducted.

These suspended losses maintain their passive status and may not be immediately deductible. The suspended nondeducted losses from an earlier year are treated as losses from a former passive activity [see §469(f)]. These previously suspended losses, however, unlike passive activity losses, are allowed against income realized from the activity after it ceases to be a passive activity.

Thus, such suspended losses are limited to the income from that specific activity but are not allowed to offset other income. Of course, the matching-of-income burden of proof is on the taxpayer.

When the taxpayer disposes of his or her entire interest in the activity in a fully taxable transaction with an unrelated party, any remaining suspended losses allocable to the activity are allowed in full.

From our ongoing example: Marilyn is carrying forward $120,000 of rental losses that were suspended from 1991 through 1993. These carry-forward losses are not immediately triggered but are either deductible against future income from this new real estate rental activity or deductible when sold.

■ Applying the Passive Loss Rules to Real Estate Professionals

Establishing Involvement in a Real Estate Business

A fairly liberal provision exists for those taxpayers involved in the real estate profession who own rental real estate. However, there are two tests that must be met if an individual is to qualify for the relief provision:

1. **50% Test.** More than 50% of the individual's personal services during the tax year must be performed in real property trades or businesses (defined below) in which the individual materially participated (deemed previously).

and

2. **750-Hour Test.** The individual must perform more than 750 hours of service in those same trades or businesses [§469 (c)(7)(B)].

Several Caveats

When this eligibility test is applied, the personal services of an employee are not counted unless the employee is also at least a 5% owner (i.e., owns more than 5% of the outstanding stock or more than 5% of the total combined voting power) [§469(c)(7)(D)(ii)].

A closely held C corporation satisfies the eligibility test if, during the tax year, more than 50% of the gross receipts of the corporation are derived from real property trades or businesses in which the corporation materially participates [§469(c)(7)(D)(i)].

Finally, this relief provision does not apply to estates, trusts, or limited partnerships owning real estate rentals. It only grants relief to individuals and closely held C corporations.

Calculating 750 Hours

An individual must perform more than 750 hours of service in the real estate rental business.

Spouse's Hours

In the case of joint returns, each spouse's personal services are taken into account separately when calculating the 50% test and the 750-hour test. But when determining "material participation," the participation of the spouse of the taxpayer is taken into account.

Stay-at-home spouses may now want to become active real estate agents. If they spend at least 750 hours cumulatively in selling and managing their family rentals, this converts the family rentals to active rentals.

A husband and wife filing a joint return meet the eligibility requirements of the provision if during the taxable year one spouse performs at least half of his or her business services in a real estate trade or business in which either spouse materially participates.

The couple does not fail the eligibility requirements if less than half of their business services, taken together, are performed in real estate trades or businesses in which either of them materially participates, provided that more than half of one spouse's business services qualify.

Remember Marilyn, the full-time real estate agent making $160,000 in commissions each year, who purchased an apartment complex, throwing off a $40,000 loss? Assume she worked 1,000 hours in the brokerage business and only an additional 100 hours managing the real estate rental. The 50% test calculation is 550 hours (1,100 × 50%) and the 750-hour calculation is 1,100 hours, which is more than the minimum required and more than the 50% minimum required hours (550 hours). Therefore, starting in 1994, all the $40,000 loss is currently deductible against her commission income.

Combining Real Estate Businesses

Real property trade or business means any real property development, redevelopment, construction, reconstruction, acquisition, conversion, rental, operation, management, leasing, or brokerage trade or business [§469(c)(7)(C)].

As a result, most of the following landlords will benefit from the new passive loss relief provision if they meet the 50% participation and the 750-hour requirements:

- Real estate builders and contractors
- Owners of rentals
- Property managers
- Participants in real estate brokerage businesses

Any hourly combination in these four businesses is permitted; for example, a taxpayer who spends 100 hours managing his or her rentals and 651 hours selling real estate exceeds the 750-hour minimum.

Brokerage Trade or Business

There is much discussion about the definition of brokerage trade or business. Do only brokers qualify, not salespersons? What about appraisers, real estate mortgage brokers, and auctioneers?

Neither the Internal Revenue Code section 469(c)(7)(C) nor the associated Conference Committee Report discusses the width or breadth of brokerage, and therefore neither specifically mentions brokers and salespersons or those in the real estate financing business (i.e., real estate mortgage bankers and brokers). Nor do they mention real estate appraisers, although under most state laws appraising is included in the definition of brokerage.

Many state licensing acts also specifically exempt auctioneers from licensure or require that auctioneers be licensed as real estate brokers. Therefore, we are left only with prior case law or state law for the definition of real estate "brokerage trade or business."

Prior Case Law

Real estate brokerages typically encompass brokers, agents, and salespersons [*Robert C. Kersey*, 66 TCM 1863]; therefore, all should qualify. People involved in brokerage firms are generally "involved in the sale, leasing, acquisition, and development of industrial and commercial real estate" [*Alfred Rice*, 38 TCM 990] and may even specialize "in sales, property management, mortgage financing, appraisals, and insurance primarily on a commission or fee basis" [*Norman A. Grant*, CA-4 *aff'g* 64-2 USTC 9586, 333 F2d 603] or simply "appraisal" [*Charles W. Yeager*, 18 TCM 192].

Brokerage businesses hire salespersons [*FB Timppins, Jr.*, 24 TCM 521], and both salespersons and brokers may be involved in the same real estate brokerage business [*Floyd Wright*, 49 TCM 906].

Another place to find the definition of real estate brokerage is state law; all 50 states have real estate brokerage licensing acts, and generally states require that real estate salespeople and brokers be licensed under the same statutory provisions [*J. G. Mendoza*, 22 TCM 528].

It is hoped and expected that future IRS rules will clarify this confusion; regulation §1.4694(h) has been reserved for these rules.

No Combination to Get Around These Rules

In spite of the new rental real estate activity relief provision, no grouping of businesses and rentals is allowed unless either is "insubstantial" in relation to the other. The problem is that the proposed regulations do not spell out "insubstantial" in relation to the other.

The lapsed temporary regulations contained two "bright-line" insubstantial tests:

1. The 2% test (i.e., if the gross rental income is less than 2% of the smaller of the property's unadjusted basis or fair market value, the rental activity is insubstantial).

and

2. The 20% test (i.e., if the rental income is less than 20% of the combined business and rental income, the rental activity is insubstantial).

It is assumed that these tests may be used to help determine if the rental is an "insubstantial" part of the business or if the business may be involved in "insubstantial" rental activities without breaking them into two activities [§1.469-4(d)].

If the grouping of rental activities with the other real property businesses is permitted by the IRS, a large tax loophole for most real estate investors exists. But such aggressive tax planning is questionable!

Back to Marilyn: If Marilyn can combine her two real property businesses (e.g., brokerage and RREA) into one activity, her $120,000 carry-forward rental losses can offset her $120,000 current brokerage income. This will bring her taxable income to zero for 1994. We seriously doubt that future IRS regulations will allow this type of activity grouping.

When Rental Is Sold for Large Profit

The question arises: What happens if the rental is sold for a large profit and the minimal annual losses were previously treated as an "active" rental loss? Rental properties treated as "active" rental losses in the year of the sale will create "active" gain at time of sale, with the result that this gain can offset only the carryover loss from that specific activity and is not available to offset any other passive losses.

Tax Planning

Any related gain on sale would not be considered passive (it stays active) unless the property were used in a passive activity for either (1) 20% of the period owned or (2) the entire 24 months prior to the date of the signing of the offer-to-purchase agreement [§1.469-2T(c)(2)(iii)].

Sandy purchases a large residential rental property with a large down payment. It throws off only a $4,000-per-year rental loss. If she meets the 50% and 750-hour tests each year, after ten years she will have deducted $40,000 of "active rental losses." If she sells the property for a $1 million profit, her gain is considered an active gain, unless she treated it as passive for 24 months prior to the signing of the offer-to-sell. Therefore, it is not available to be used against her other "limited partnership" passive losses.

■ Conclusion

Real estate agents, contractors, and developers who own real estate should be overjoyed over the return of the tax benefits previously enjoyed by everyone before 1987! But Congress exacted a price: to use this relief provision requires a meticulous time log and a few extra hours with a tax preparer!

■ Chapter 4 Review Questions

1. Passive losses can be subtracted from the tax-payer's other active income.
   a. True
   b. False

2. A real estate investor can meet the "material" participation rule by spending more than 500 hours a year managing and operating an apartment building.
   a. True
   b. False

3. An investor can wash windows on his apartment building to prove "material participation."
   a. True
   b. False

4. It is a wise idea for landlords to keep careful time logs when managing their investment properties.
   a. True
   b. False

5. A person can claim to be in real estate if he or she works more than 750 hours and more than 50% of this time is spent on real estate listing and selling.
   a. True
   b. False

6. Taxpayers who manage rental properties and sell real estate can deduct rental losses from their commission income.
   a. True
   b. False

7. A husband-and-wife team who are both active real estate agents and who manage their own property can combine their hours to materially participate.
   a. True
   b. False

8. Real estate rentals can be lumped together as a single activity, and these groupings can be changed from year to year.
   a. True
   b. False

9. Owners of vacation condominium rentals generally avoid the passive loss limitations.
   a. True
   b. False

10. Middle-income taxpayers can deduct up to $50,000 of rental losses from their income.
    a. True
    b. False

Office-in-Home Rules

learning objectives

Upon completing this chapter, you will be able to:

- summarize the three criteria to establish an office-in-home deduction;

- define principal place of business;

- discuss which transportation costs may be converted to business mileage;

- cite examples of direct and indirect expenses that are used to calculate the office-in-home deduction; and

- calculate the office-in-home deduction.

■ Key Terms

depreciation recapture	indirect expenses	transportation expenses
direct expenses	principal place of business	

■ Overview

A recent nontraditional trend in the business community finds many taxpayers working out of their personal residences. When a portion of a home is used for business purposes, a percentage of the total housing costs of these normally non-deductible personal expenses may be deducted as business expenses by a taxpayer who is an individual or an S corporation.

Congress has found it necessary to prevent taxpayers from misusing the office-in-home deduction, so now stringent "exclusive, regular, and principal" rules must be followed before this deduction is permitted. Many real estate licensees and others, who do a fair amount of work from their homes, often are not permitted to take this deduction. This chapter explains these rules with examples.

■ What Are the Office-in-Home Requirements?

To qualify for a home-office deduction, the portion of a home that is used for business must meet all of the following three criteria:

1. It must be used *exclusively* for business.
2. It must be used on a *regular basis* for business activity.
3. It must be *principally* used for at least one of the following business activities:

   a. As the principal place of business for any trade or business conducted by the taxpayer;

   or

   b. As a place of business for meeting or dealing with patients, clients, or customers in the ordinary course of business;

   or

   c. In connection with the taxpayer's trade or business if the taxpayer is using a separate structure that is not attached to the dwelling [§280A(c)(1)].

These rules make personal investment activities (e.g., reading financial periodicals, clipping bond coupons, etc.) ineligible for home-office deductions, as they do not rise to the level of a "business" activity [*J. A. Moller*, CA-FC 83-2 USTC ¶9698].

Employee Working at Home

In the case of a home office used by an employee, the employee must also establish that the home office is for the convenience of his or her employer [§280A(c)(1)].

Tax Tip! If an employee works from home, the home office is deductible only if such exclusive use is for the convenience of the employer. The question of whether an employee chose not to use suitable space made available by the employer for administrative activities would be relevant to determining whether the "convenience of the employer" test is satisfied [§280A(c)].

Renting a Room to Employer

A home-office deduction is barred when an employee leases a portion of his or her home to the employer. This rule also extends to an independent contractor who attempts to lease to the party for whom he or she performs services (e.g., a real estate licensee should not lease office space located at home to his or her broker/owner) [§280A(c)(6)].

Room Exclusively Used for Business

To qualify for use of the home office deduction, there must be a specific room or area that is set aside and used exclusively (no personal use during the year, including storage of personal items) on a regular basis as the principal place of any business. The exclusive rule will be met only if there is no use of the business portion of the dwelling unit at any time during the year other than for qualified business purposes.

The mere absence of a wall, partition, curtain, or the like does not negate this deduction but does raise the level of inquiry by the IRS agent. Also, the act of walking through the home office to another room is not a violation of this rule [PR§1.280A-2(g); *Weightman*, 42 TCM 104, 1981-301; §1.280A(g)(1); *C. D. Hughes*, 41 TCM 1153, 1981-140].

Work from one business brought home (i.e., college professor correcting student tests) and taken into the office-in-home (that was the sole office of the professor's other business of being an actor) taints the room by making it a nonexclusive use and therefore a nonbusiness room [*A. W. Hamacher v. Comm.*, 94TC 348, No. 21].

Joan, a real estate agent, also operates an advertising agency from her personal residence. She may not make real estate brokerage calls from her advertising agency home office.

Operating Two or More Businesses from Same Home Office

The judge in *Hamacher* made clear that two businesses may be exclusively operated out of the same office-in-home. But each activity must satisfy all the statutory requirements. For example, real estate brokers or business persons with a home office for managing property owned by themselves or others (e.g., a second business as a property manager) may be able to deduct an office-in-home.

If any deduction, such as a home office, is first determined personal and, hence, nondeductible, the taxpayer cannot subsequently deduct any business office expenses. Unfortunately, there is not a clear dividing line between (a) deductible business expenses that render passing personal benefits, and (b) nondeductible personal expenses that incidentally benefit business purposes [*S. A. Bodzin*, CA-4, 75-1 USTC ¶9190].

Exclusive Rule Exceptions: Day Care and Inventory Storage

The exclusive use requirement does not apply when the home is used for qualified day care of children, handicapped, or the elderly, nor does it apply to wholesale or retail sellers regularly storing inventory in the home (e.g., part-time Mary Kay or Shakley salespeople) and solely working out of their homes [§.280A(c)(4); §280A(c)(2); §1.280A-2(e)].

Regular Use

Even though no home-office case specifically defines regular use, this test implies that the home office is being used systematically throughout the year. Occasional or incidental business use of the home office will not be sufficient even though the room meets the exclusivity requirement.

Patients, Clients, or Customers

If a taxpayer, through his or her normal course of business, meets or deals with patients, clients, or customers in his or her home, the deduction will not be denied as long as the space is used exclusively and regularly for these business activities. This exception applies even though the taxpayer may carry on business at another location. The IRS emphasizes that this exception applies only when the taxpayer is actually visited by clients or patients and will not apply to a room where only phone calls are received [§280A(c)(1)(B); IRS Pub. 587, p. 3].

The preceding qualifies doctors, dentists, attorneys, barbers, therapists, beauticians, and even owners of small grocery stores who operate their businesses from their homes.

Separate Structures

Tax Tip! Separate structures could include a guest cottage used as a dentist's office or a separate garage converted into an artist's studio.

This exception applies to the freestanding structure apart from the taxpayer's residence if such structure is used exclusively and regularly in the taxpayer's trade or business. It is not necessary for the taxpayer to establish that the structure is his or her principal place of business or that it is a place where he or she meets patients, clients, or customers [§280A(c)(l)(C)].

What Defines Principal Place of Business?

Before 1997, neither the Internal Revenue Code nor Congressional Committee reports explained what was meant by "principal place of business," thus leaving it to the administrative and judicial branches for the definition. They did, much to the taxpayer's chagrin, in *Commissioner v. Soliman*, 113 SCT 701 (1993); IRS Notice 93-12; and Rev. Rul. 94-24.

Essentially, in *Soliman*, the Supreme Court and the IRS very strictly ruled that the principal place of business is where "client contact" occurs, as that is where the primary income-generation functions are performed. This eliminated approximately 95% of the previously deducted home offices. The legislative branch corrected this inequitable result, but only effective for tax returns filed starting in 1999.

Applying the Principal Place of Business Test

If the taxpayer has only one place of business, this is considered the taxpayer's "regular" place of business, a location deemed superior to a principal place of business. If this regular place of business is in the home, the taxpayer would have a deductible office-in-home, assuming the exclusive and regular requirements are met.

IRS Example:

Danny is a self-employed author who uses a home office to write. He spends 30 to 35 hours of his work time per week writing in his home office. Danny also spends another 10 to 15 hours of his work time per week at other locations conducting research, meeting with his publishers, and attending promotional events.

The essence of Danny's trade or business as an author is writing. Danny's research, meetings with publishers and attendance at promotional events, while essential, are less important and take less time than his writing. Therefore, Danny's office in the home is his principal place of business, and he can deduct expenses for the business use of the home [Rev. Rul. 94-24].

Home-Office Definition Expanded

To reverse the *Soliman* decision, Congress created a simple, two-step test to determine if the home office is the taxpayer's principal place of business.

Parity

This legislative correction gives small home-based businesses parity with those companies that choose to rent space and deduct the lease payments. The claim is also made that it recognizes advances in technology that encourage operating a home-based business and that also help cut down on commuting, thus conserving energy, provide a financial boost to these businesses; help create jobs; and are even pro-family (at last, a tax law with a moral purpose).

Two Tests

A home office qualifies as the taxpayer's "principal place of business" if

1. the home office is used by the taxpayer for administrative or management activities of any trade or business of the taxpayer

and

2. there is no other fixed location of the trade or business where the taxpayer conducts substantial administrative or management activities of the trade or business [new §280A(c)(1) flush language and effective for tax years after December 31, 1998].

Tax Planning

This liberal expansion allows the office deduction for the vast majority of the estimated 34 million business persons who work out of their homes, such as

- home-based employees who telecommunicate to the main office;
- doctors who perform their duties in hospitals but need to do their billings from their home office;
- outside salespeople who call at the customer's place of business;
- professional speakers who prepare at home but deliver the presentation at hotels and convention centers; and
- plumbers and other tradespeople who perform their duties at job sites away from the shop.

Tax Tip! Regular and Exclusive Requirements Still in Effect: The home-office deduction is allowed only if the office is also exclusively used on a regular basis as a place of business by the taxpayer.

Many taxpayers who have a second business conducted out of their home will be able to deduct their traveling to and from their "home office" to their main office (previously considered nondeductible commuting mileage) under this expanded definition. This topic is discussed later in this chapter.

The House Committee Report provides the following examples of the types of taxpayers who will be able to use this new, expanded definition of principal place of business.

- Taxpayers who carry out administrative or management activities at sites that are not fixed locations of the business (e.g., in a car or hotel room), in addition to performing those same activities in their home office
- Taxpayers who do not conduct substantial administrative or management activities at a fixed location other than the home office, even if administrative or management activities (e.g., billing activities) are performed by other people at other locations
- Taxpayers who conduct some administrative or management activities at a fixed location of the business outside the home, so long as the administrative or management activities conducted at any fixed location of the business outside the home are not substantial (e.g., the taxpayer occasionally does minimal paperwork at another fixed location of the business)
- Taxpayers who conduct substantial nonadministrative or nonmanagement business activities at a fixed location of the business outside the home office (e.g., meeting with or providing services to customers, clients, or patients at a fixed location of the business away from the home office)

■ Taxpayers who in fact do not perform substantial administrative or management activities at any fixed location of the business away from home (i.e., they do all this work at home) will find the second requirement satisfied. This is true regardless of whether or not the taxpayer opted not to use an office away from home that was available for the conduct of such activities.

Therefore, taxpayers who perform administrative or management activities for their trade or business at places other than the home office are not automatically prohibited from taking this deduction. Additionally, in cases where a taxpayer's use of a home office does not satisfy the two-part test, the taxpayer nevertheless may be able to claim a home-office deduction under the present-law "principal place of business" exception or any other provision of §280A.

■ What about Transportation Expenses from a Home Office?

Commuting from a Home Office

A deductible home office often converts nondeductible commuting mileage to business mileage, if the taxpayer's home office is the principal place of business. Each business trip from home is considered a deductible transportation expense when the taxpayer is traveling between different business locations. Because this may amount to a substantial annual tax deduction, it may pay to have an office-in-home.

However, if the principal office is at another location (e.g., a real estate office located downtown), the mileage from the nonbusiness-use residence to the first business location is a nondeductible commuting trip [Rev. Rul. 190; Rev. Rul. 55-109]. This liberalized definition of a principal place of business allows many more taxpayers to deduct their "commuting" costs. Financially, this is a potentially larger deduction for most taxpayers than the office-in-home deduction.

Marianne is a real estate broker who is also a professional singer at the local jazz club. As she is the administrative manager of the brokerage firm, with a corner office, any brokerage office-in-home activities would not be deductible. But as she has no other administrative office for her singing business, and as she conducts substantial nonadministrative and nonmanagerial business activities at a fixed location other than at the home office, her musical home office qualifies.

Therefore, if every morning she first performs work duties at her home office before going to her second job site, she may be able to deduct the mileage between her home and her downtown brokerage office. But, if she has only one job, the trip from home to the real estate office is a nondeductible commuting trip.

Nondeductible Office-in-Home and the Transportation Deduction

It is not clear whether a taxpayer can call a nondeductible office-in-home a "principal place of business" and retain the transportation deduction by arguing that he or she is traveling between two places of business. The Tax Court, in one disturbing anti-taxpayer case, concluded "because the automobile expenses were incurred in commuting to and from a home office which does not qualify under section 280A(c)(1), the automobile expenses are not deductible" [*A. W. Hamacher v. Comm.*, 94TC 348, No. 21]. It is not known if the argument was made that a non-deductible office may still be a principal place of business, the argument successfully used in the next case.

Charles Walker did not establish that his residence was his "principal place of business" (a requirement to establish a deductible home office), but he did convince the court that his home was a "regular place of business" (a more liberal requirement). As Charles was "going between two specific business locations," the mileage between his home and his next business location was a deductible business expense [Rev. Rul. 55-109, 1955-1C.B. 261].

Charles kept daily records showing that he spent approximately seven hours per week in the workshop adjacent to his residence maintaining and repairing his equipment even though no office-in-home deduction was taken. The court found that even though a taxpayer is not deducting (or cannot deduct) an office-in-home, this does not negate the fact that the office in the home is a regular place of business [Charles W. Walker and Cathe R. Walker v. Comm., 101 T.C. 537 (1993)].

The IRS disagrees with Walker and in Rev. Rul. 94-47, the IRS states that there are only two situations in which a transportation deduction is allowed for expenses incurred in traveling between a residence and a temporary place of business in the same metropolitan area. These cases are

1. where the taxpayer also has a regular place of business that is not located at the taxpayer's residence or
2. where the taxpayer's residence is his or her principal place of business.

Accounting for Home-Office Expenses More Difficult

When income tax Form 1040, Schedule C, is filed, the taxpayer is instructed to attach Form 8829, Expenses for Business Use of Your Home. The reason for Form 8829 is apparent. The IRS wants to prevent the home-office deduction from being hidden under some other heading (e.g., office expenses, miscellaneous expenses, or spread throughout Schedule C as interest, taxes, and utilities). In addition, the agency wants to determine if the taxpayer is properly deducting these expenses.

Another reason for Form 8829 is that Congress believes taxpayers are abusing the office-in-home deduction and asked the IRS to analyze the potential misuse. The IRS wants to determine if the taxpayer is complying with the home-office limitations and if the calculation is being done correctly.

Even though an office-in-home deduction may act as a red flag for audit, taxpayers should take all legitimate deductions. A red flag does not mean an audit is imminent. This material is designed to examine proper tax reporting, keeping in mind the philosophy of eminent jurist Learned Hand, who said that "tax avoidance is a constitutional right." On the other hand, tax *evasion* can lead to prison.

■ What Is the Office-in-Home Calculation?

When a portion of the taxpayer's personal home is used for business purposes, the fill-in-the-blank worksheet shown as Figure 5.1 helps determine the business deduction for the office-in-home.

Calculating the Allowable Home-Office Deduction

Two types of expenses, direct and indirect, are deducted on Form 8829 when the home is used for business purposes. Any other expenses, such as salaries, supplies, and business telephone expenses, are deductible elsewhere on Schedule C and should not be entered on Form 8829.

Direct Expenses

These expenses benefit only the actual office itself, such as painting or repairs made to the specific area or room used for business. All of these expenses (100%) are entered on the appropriate expense line in column (a) of Form 8829.

Indirect Expenses

These expenses are for keeping up and running the entire home, for example, interest, taxes, roof repairs, and utilities. They benefit both the business and personal parts of the home. Generally, 100% of these expenses are entered on the appropriate expense line in column (b) of Form 8829, totaled and deductible only to the extent of the business percentage.

Exception

If the business percentage of an indirect expense is more accurately determined separately, it is to be included as a direct expense. For example, if the electricity of the home office is on a separate meter or if the taxes are itemized between business personal property and home personal property, these normally indirect expenses should be considered direct expenses.

Calculation of Business Percentage

Previously, the business percentage was determined either by dividing the square footage of the office-in-home by the total square footage of the home (e.g., 200-square-foot office ÷ 3,000 square-foot-home = 6.67%) or by dividing the office room by the number of rooms in the house (e.g., 1-room office ÷ 10-room home = 10%) and using the percentage most advantageous to the taxpayer.

Now the taxpayer must use only the square-footage method because the room-by-room allocation has been rejected by the courts. According to the newly released instruction of Form 8829, the room-by-room method is available only if "the rooms in the house are all about the same size" (i.e., each bathroom is the same size as the living room, etc.).

Edward Andrews claimed a deduction based on the ratio of rooms in the house, but the court determined that the home-office expenses should more reasonably be allocated on a square-footage basis [E. W. Andrews v. Comm., TC Memo. 1990-391].

Figure 5.1 | Office-In-Home Deduction Calculation

```
┌─────────────────────────────────────────────────────────────┐
│                                                               │
│        ╭───────────────────────────────────────────╮         │
│        │   Office-in-Home Deduction Calculation     │         │
│        ╰───────────────────────────────────────────╯         │
│                         Total        Personal        Sched. A* │
│                        Expense         Use           Deduction │
│   Casualty Losses      $_____   x  _____%  =  $_____           │
│   Mortgage Interest    $_____   x  _____%  =  $_____           │
│   Property Taxes       $_____   x  _____%  =  $_____           │
│   Insurance            $_____                                  │
│   Utilities            $_____                                  │
│   Repairs & Maintenance $_____                                 │
│   Janitor or Maid Service $_____                               │
│   Depreciation (39 years) $_____                               │
│   Mortgage Interest    $_____     Business      Home Office    │
│   ─────────────────────────        Use         Deduction†     │
│   Total Expenses       $_____   x  _____%  =  $_____           │
│     * Deduct on Schedule A, Personal 1040   † Subject to §280A(c) │
└─────────────────────────────────────────────────────────────┘
```

Limitation on Home-Office Deduction—No Losses

A home-office deduction is not allowed to the extent that it creates or increases a net loss of a business. Any disallowed deduction is carried over to the next tax year, subject to the same limits in the carryover years, whether or not the dwelling unit is used as a residence during the tax year. Any unused carryover amounts are lost if the business closes.

For administrative purposes only, the IRS does allow the office-in-home deduction to create or increase a loss if that loss is created solely by otherwise deductible home mortgage interest and tax deduction. The following example demonstrates this exception, which increases the allowable loss from zero to a negative $1,000, illustrating the office-in-home deduction as well as the proper use of Form 8829 and Schedule C (see examples at the end of this chapter).

> *Jill, a real estate agent, operates an advertising agency from her 2,000-square-foot home and makes qualified business use of a 500-square-foot home office, i.e., a 25% business use (see Figure 5.2).*

Home Office Creates No Gain When Residence Is Sold

No allocation of gain is required if both the residential and nonresidential portions of the property are within the same dwelling unit. The fact that a residence is rented or is used partially for business (i.e., a home office) at the time of sale does not disqualify the gain attributable to the business use, other than depreciation recapture, from the $250,000/$500,000 exclusion. But, the §121 exclusion will not apply to the gain allocable to any portion of property sold or exchanged with respect to which a taxpayer does not satisfy the use requirement if the nonresidential portion is separate from the dwelling unit [§1.121-1(e)(1)]. The final regu-

Figure 5.2 | Profit or Loss Calculation

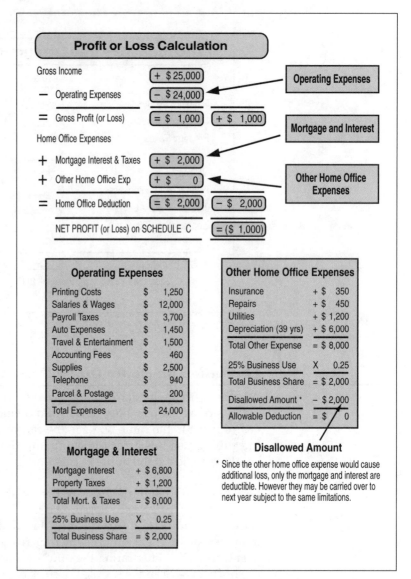

lations provide that the term *dwelling unit* has the same meaning as in §280A(f)(1), but does not include appurtenant structures or other property [§1.121-1(e)(2)].

Kate sells her personal residence, which contains her deductible office-in-home, for a $100,000 gain. She estimates that the office occupies 10% of her home. She can exclude the entire $100,000 gain other than the depreciation recapture of $2,000. The $10,000 gain associated with the office-in-home is not taxable [§1.121-1(e)(4), Ex. 5 & 6

	Total	Residence	Office-in-Home
Sales Price	$300,000	$270,000	$30,000
Original Cost	200,000	180,000	20,000
Less Depreciation	− 2,000	- 0 -	− 2,000
Adjusted Basis	198,000	180,000	18,000
Total Gain	102,000	90,000	12,000
§121 Exclusion	100,000	90,000	12,000
Total Gain	2,000	90,000 (Excludable)	2,000 (Taxable)

Depreciation Taken after May 6, 1997, Must Be Recaptured

Tax Tip! An office-in-home can be converted back to personal use only after two years of personal use in a five-year period.

Any gain attributable to depreciation taken after May 6, 1997, with respect to the prior rental or business use of the principal residence must be recognized in the year of the sale (but interestingly not an exchange) [§121(d)(5)].

Therefore, 65.753% of the 1997 depreciation must be recaptured. The period of May 7 through December 31, 1997, is 240 days.

Kim purchased a home on May 7, 1997, and sold it for a $30,000 profit on December 31, 1999. The accumulated depreciation on her office-in-home was $700. Therefore, $29,300 gain is excluded by §121 but the $700 must be reported on Form 4797 as depreciation recapture income, assuming the home office was converted back to personal use no later than December 31, 1997 (see Figure 5.2).

■ Conclusion

With proper tax planning, an office-in-home deduction can be quite beneficial for those taxpayers who are working from their homes. This deduction is not available for most real estate licensees who use an office supplied by their broker.

On the other hand, those licensees who also have another business (such as a property management agency) located in their homes that is used exclusively and on a regular basis as a principal place of business may find that commuting mileage might be converted to business mileage.

Clearly Congress is keeping close tabs on the office-in-home issue, so the taxpayer who decides to use this deduction should keep careful records and logs of time.

■ Chapter 5 Review Questions

1. An employee can rent a room in his house to his employer in order to qualify for a home office deduction.

   a. True

   b. False

2. Home-based caretakers of children do not have to set aside a portion of their homes just for the children.

   a. True

   b. False

3. A real estate licensee can create an office in his or her home and deduct those expenses as an office-in-home, even though the licensee regularly uses an office supplied by the broker.

   a. True

   b. False

4. The IRS generally requires that the home-office deduction be based on square footage actually used.

   a. True

   b. False

5. When a home is sold, the percentage that was used as an office in the same dwelling unit must be reported as the sale of a taxable office, and taxes must be paid on this gain.

   a. True

   b. False

6. A home office in an expensive home can be used to create a loss for the business.

   a. True

   b. False

7. For tax purposes, an office-in-home can never be converted back to personal use.

   a. True

   b. False

8. An office-in-home can be utilized as a spare bedroom and still qualify for the tax deduction.

   a. True

   b. False

9. Two businesses may be operated out of the same home office, if both qualify as independent businesses.

   a. True

   b. False

10. Expenses for a separate building used for business purposes will qualify for a tax deduction without establishing that the building is the principal place of business.

    a. True

    b. False

chapter six

Case Studies

The following Case Studies apply basic concepts from this course to "real-life" situations. Please read each Case Study carefully, then answer the questions and include your comments.

case study | **Chapter 1 Home Mortgage Interest Deduction**

Gary Lofstrum and Scott Jaswal have just finished a round of golf and are sitting in the clubhouse discussing their upcoming business plans. Gary's father died recently and Gary inherited the family's $300,000 home in the St. Louis area. His father had paid off the mortgage some time ago. Gary has just purchased a $300,000 second home in Portland, Oregon, with a bank loan. He used the St. Louis home as collateral for the loan.

Scott just completed purchase of a $200,000 principal residence in Key West with a down payment of $50,000. He now wants to borrow funds to buy a $100,000 yacht and use his Key West home as security for the loan in order to convert a nondeductible personal loan to a deductible qualified-residence interest loan.

1. Gary cannot deduct the interest on the bank loan for his home in Portland because

   a. a second home does not usually qualify as a residence for tax purposes.

   b. the Portland home is in a different state from his St. Louis home.

   c. the Portland home is not "specific security" for payment of the loan.

   d. he never had any acquisition debt in the St. Louis home.

2. Scott will not qualify for a $100,000 home equity loan on the yacht because

   a. interest on a loan used to buy personal property can never be deductible.

   b. he has insufficient equity in his home.

   c. he has insufficient acquisition debt.

   d. a home equity loan cannot be used for purchase of personal property.

Student Comments

Please provide your comments regarding the basic principle(s) addressed in this case study, and its relevance to the subject matter generally:

_____

_____

_____

_____

_____

case study   **Chapter 2 Taxation of Profit**

Terri Lafferty has just sold a farmhouse and farm in central Minnesota that she purchased and rehabbed 15 years ago. She bought the property for $150,000. She spent $200,000 to rehab the damaged farmhouse and $50,000 to build a combination garage-art studio. She never claimed any depreciation deductions. She estimates she spent about $2,000 a year in general maintenance. She sold the property for $900,000. She paid a 7% commission and an additional $10,000 in selling expenses.

Terri doesn't know much about real estate taxes, so she wants to learn how her gains or losses are computed.

1. The simplest explanation of the "gain or loss" formula is

    a. sales price minus original price or basis.

    b. sales price minus improvements or original cost.

    c. net selling price minus adjusted basis.

    d. net selling price plus original cost minus adjusted basis.

2. Which of the following expenditures usually does NOT increase the adjusted basis of a property?

    a. Purchase expenses

    b. Construction costs

    c. Costs of rebuilding damaged property

    d. Maintenance repairs

Student Comments

Please provide your comments regarding the basic principle(s) addressed in this case study, and its relevance to the subject matter generally:

_____

_____

_____

_____

Chapter 3 Exclusion Rule

Mark and Paula Clarkson own a ranch house in Laramie, Wyoming. Mark purchased the house from his parents four years ago when they moved to a retirement community several miles away. At the time Mark and Paula were employed as teachers at the community high school.

A year later Mark was appointed to a college teaching position at the University of Nebraska in Lincoln. He and Paula purchased a mobile home to live in while Mark taught and Paula worked as a freelance journalist at the *Lincoln Star.* Mark knew his teaching and research duties would require frequent travel to Denver, so he and Paula also purchased a condominium in downtown Denver. The research work in Denver consumes a substantial portion, but not a majority of Mark's time, so Paula travels with him when he stays in Denver. The Clarksons return to their Laramie ranch house as often as possible because Mark's parents like to visit them in the family home.

The Clarksons have owned three homes for the last three years, and want to sell or rent two of the properties. If they sell, they want to gain the maximum benefit of the new exclusion of gain rule.

1. The Clarksons' principal residence for tax purposes probably is the

    a. mobile home in Lincoln, because that is the home in the area where they work.

    b. condominium in Denver, because that is where they now spend a substantial amount of their time.

    c. ranch house in Wyoming, because that is where they return when not working.

    d. They have no principal residence.

2. Which of the following criteria does NOT affect whether the Clarksons will qualify under the exclusion rule to report zero taxable gain on the sale of their principal residence?

    a. Their net gain is less than or equal to $500,000.

    b. They file a joint tax return for the taxable year of the sale.

    c. They reinvest the sales proceeds in another home within 24 months.

    d. They have not used the exclusion within the last two years.

Student Comments

Please provide your comments regarding the basic principle(s) addressed in this case study, and its relevance to the subject matter generally:

_____

_____

_____

_____

_____

case study	**Chapter 4 Applying the Passive Loss Rules to Real Estate Professionals**

Paul Moreno is a prominent heart surgeon in Atlanta who earns $600,000 a year. He invests in a variety of limited partnerships, including real estate. Over the past several years he has lost substantial amounts of money through his real estate investments.

Paul's younger brother, Jerry, is an advertising executive earning $200,000 a year. Jerry wants to invest in the rental real estate market. Paul has warned him about the severity of the passive loss rule, but Jerry thinks he can avoid that problem if he helps manage the rental real estate activities in which he invests.

1. Paul can apply the losses from his passive real estate investment activities against the income from his

    a. passive activities and all other sources combined.

    b. passive activities and salary combined.

    c. passive activities and investments combined.

    d. passive activities only.

2. Which of the following tests probably would NOT enable Jerry to meet the material participation rule for his rental real estate activities?

    a. Managing and operating the business for more than 500 hours

    b. Regularly studying and reviewing all financial and legal documents

    c. Doing substantially all of the managing and operating of the business

    d. Working more than 100 hours with no one else participating more than the landlord

Student Comments

Please provide your comments regarding the basic principle(s) addressed in this case study, and its relevance to the subject matter generally:

_____

_____

_____

_____

_____

| **case study** | **Chapter 5 Office-in-Home Rules** |

Sonja Adjani has worked as a real estate broker for Decker Properties in Albuquerque, New Mexico, for nearly ten years. She wants to spend more time with her children, but does not want to give up the success she has achieved in real estate. She plans to set up a home office from which she would continue to conduct her real estate practice.

The principals at Decker want Sonja to continue working for them and are willing to let her work from her home office occasionally. But they want her to maintain a significant presence in their main office.

Sonja's husband, Jan, has suggested she leave Decker and start a private real estate practice using her home office full-time. He thinks the potential tax deductions will help improve their financial situation.

1. If Sonja agrees to stay with Decker, she probably will not be able to deduct expenses for her home office because she is NOT using it

   a. exclusively for business.

   b. on a regular basis for business activity.

   c. as her principal place of business.

   d. as her legal place of business.

2. Sonja will NOT be able to use her full home-office deduction if

   a. direct expenses exceed indirect expenses.

   b. the deduction creates or increases a net loss of her business.

   c. the office is less than 25% of the home's square footage.

   d. the office is used primarily for client meetings.

Student Comments

Please provide your comments regarding the basic principle(s) addressed in this case study, and its relevance to the subject matter generally:

_____

_____

_____

_____

_____

The Internet is an excellent source of information, especially for technical and government-related issues. Above is a sample of the Internal Revenue Service Home Page. Subsequent Web pages provide specific tax law and tax case information. Below are Internet addresses (URLs) for several tax-related Web sites.

IRS Home Page   *www.irs.gov*

IRS Tax Professionals   *www.irs.gov/ taxpros/index.html (tax information for tax professionals)*

IRS Tax Topics   *www.irs.gov/taxtopics/ index.html (main index of tax topics' categories)*

IRS Forms   *www.irs.gov/formspubs/ toprequests.html (top requested forms and publications)*

IRS (Form 553, Tax Changes)   *www.irs.gov/pub/irs-pdf/p553.pdf (highlights of 2003 tax changes)*

Tax and Accounting   *www/taxsites.com/federal.html*

Tax Links   *www.el.com/elinks/taxes/ (collection of links to tax-related Web sites on the Internet)*

Tax Tips   *www.smbiz.com (tax and management guidance for small and medium sized businesses)*

Tax Watch   *www.riahome.com/taxwatch/ (key legislative developments)*

Chapter 1 Review Questions

1. *F* (1)   Home mortgage interest remains fully deductible to arrive at taxable income.

2. *T* (2)

3. *T* (13)

4. *T* (1)

5. *F* (2)   Acquisition debt is that still owed before refinancing. When paid down or paid off, it cannot be reinstated. If the refinancing includes substantial improvements to the property, that interest may be deductible.

6. *F* (7)   The taxpayer may designate each year which residence is to be treated as the second residence. This election does not apply to the principal residence.

7. *F* (9)   The newly married couple will have one principal residence and one "second dwelling" unit.

8. *T* (11)

9. *F* (13)   Charges for lender's services are not interest and are not currently deductible.

10. *F* (2)   The combined amount of acquisition indebtedness for principal and second residences is up to $1 million.

Chapter 2 Review Questions

1. *T* (23)

2. *F* (23)   Any mortgage taken over (assumption or "subject to") must be figured in to the total sale price.

3. *F* (25)   Prorated items may not be counted as selling expenses because they are ongoing costs associated with ownership, not incurred because of the sale.

4. *T* (26)

5. *T* (30)

6. *T* (22, 25)

7. *F* (20)   Sale price minus original price or basis equals gain or loss. Basis is increased by improvements and may be decreased by accumulated depreciation, thus affecting gain or loss.

8. *F* (24)   The buyer and seller must use the same selling price. Selling price for tax purposes includes total assets transferred from the seller to the buyer, regardless of whether they are mentioned in the sales contract.

9. *F* (20)   Property received by gift or inheritance need not be reported because no sale or exchange took place.

10. *T* (28)   Repair costs may be deducted currently. Capital expenditures may not be deducted but must be recovered through annual expenses (called *depreciation deductions*) taken over the useful life of depreciable property.

Chapter 3 Review Questions

1. *F* (34)   This rule has been eliminated.
2. *T* (37)
3. *T* (39)
4. *F* (34)   A taxpayer may claim only one principal residence; the other may be a "second" dwelling.
5. *T* (40)
6. *T* (40)
7. *T* (45)
8. *F* (45)   The law permits the home to be rented three out of the past five years.
9. *F* (46)   Any loss on the sale of a personal residence is nondeductible.
10. *T* (48)

Chapter 4 Review Questions

1. *F* (52)   Passive losses may not be deducted against other income.
2. *T* (54)
3. *F* (55)   The owner must perform work usually done by owners and/or managers.
4. *T* (54)
5. *T* (57)
6. *T* (53)
7. *T* (57)
8. *F* (55)   Once grouped, they will be treated as a single rental activity for years to come.
9. *F* (56)   Most vacation condominium rentals are passive businesses because they don't qualify as rentals and the owners don't materially participate in the management of the condo.
10. *F* (52)   Middle-income taxpayers can deduct up to $25,000 of rental losses from "actively managed" real estate.

Chapter 5 Review Questions

1. *F* (64)   Real estate agents cannot rent a room of their home to their employer for tax reasons.
2. *T* (65)
3. *F* (65)   Because brokers provide office space, most real estate agents cannot take this deduction.
4. *T* (70)
5. *F* (71)
6. *F* (71)   A home-office deduction is not allowed to create or increase a net business loss.
7. *F* (73)   It takes two years to convert to personal use.
8. *F* (64)   No personal use during the year is permitted, including storage of personal items.
9. *T* (65)
10. *T* (65)

Chapter 6 Case Studies

Case Study: Chapter 1: Home Mortgage Interest Deduction

1. *c* (9)   The Portland home is not "specific security" for payment of the loan.

2. *b* (10)   He has insufficient equity in his home.

Case Study: Chapter 2: Taxation of Profit

1. *a* (20)   Sales price minus original price is the simplest explanation.

2. *d* (28)   Maintenance repairs

Case Study: Chapter 3: Exclusion Rule

1. *a* (34)   The mobile home in Lincoln is the home in the area where they work.

2. *c* (35)   They reinvest the sales proceeds into another home within 24 months.

Case Study: Chapter 4: Applying the Passive Loss Rules

1. *d* (52)   Passive activities only

2. *b* (54)   Regularly studying and reviewing all financial and legal documents

Case Study: Chapter 5: Office-in-Home Rules

1. *c* (64)   Principally for business

2. *b* (66)   The deduction creates a net loss of a business.

Acquisition indebtedness Debt that is incurred to acquire, construct, or substantially improve a taxpayer's principal or second residence and that is secured by the property.

Adjusted basis The original cost (purchase price plus buying expenses) of property (or basis, if the owner didn't buy the property), plus the value of improvements made on the property, minus depreciation and losses taken while owning it.

Buying expenses All expenses incurred to complete the purchase transaction. If a capital gain is realized on the sale, the buying expenses reduce the gain.

Capital expenditure Amount paid to (1) acquire property with a useful life in excess of one year, or (2) permanently improve property.

Cooperative A residential multiunit building whose title is held by a trust or corporation that is owned by and operated for the benefit of persons living within the building, who are the beneficial owners of the trust or stockholders of the corporation, each possessing a proprietary lease.

Depreciation A method of matching income and related expenses. Depreciation is intended to recognize the decrease in value caused by wear and tear, outdated interior improvements, and neighborhood problems. Land itself may never be depreciated, only the improvements.

Direct expenses For the office-in-home deduction, expenses that benefit only the actual office itself, such as painting or repairs made to the specific area or room used for business.

Dwelling unit A house, apartment, condominium, mobile home, boat, or similar property. A dwelling unit does not include personal property such as furniture or a television that is not a fixture.

Fair market value The price at which the property would change hands between a willing buyer and a willing seller, provided that neither was under any extraordinary pressure to buy or sell.

Form 8829 The IRS form used to figure the allowable expenses for business use of the taxpayer's home on Schedule C (Form 1040) and any carryover to next year of any expenses not deductible in the current month.

Home equity indebtedness Debt (other than acquisition indebtedness) that is secured by the taxpayer's principal or second residence and does not exceed fair market value of the qualified residence.

Indirect expenses For the office-in-home deduction, expenses for keeping up and running the entire home, such as interest, taxes, roof repairs, and utilities. They benefit both the business and personal parts of the home.

Interest Anything paid as compensation for the use of money.

Judgment The formal decision of a court regarding the respective rights and claims of the parties to an action or suit. After a judgment has been entered and recorded with the county recorder, it usually becomes a general lien on the property of the defendant.

Material participation Participation in a trade or business activity on a "regular, continuous, and substantial" basis.

Mechanic's lien A statutory lien created in favor of contractors, laborers, and materialmen who have performed work or furnished materials in the erection or repair of a building.

Option The right to buy real property in the future instead of buying the property right now, usually paying only a small fraction of the total purchase price for this future right.

Personal property Items, called *chattels*, that do not fit into the definition of real property; movable objects.

Points A loan fee that is expressed as a percentage. One point is one percent of the loan amount.

Principal place of business The home office used by the taxpayer for administrative or management activities of any trade or business of the taxpayer where there is no other fixed location of the trade or business where the taxpayer conducts substantial administrative or management activities of the trade or business.

Principal residence Normally, the home in the area where the taxpayer works. Or, if the taxpayer is not working, it is where the taxpayer spends the most amount of time, votes, pays taxes, files his or her tax return, etc.

Qualified residence The taxpayer's principal residence and/or the taxpayer's second residence.

Remainder interest The remnant of an estate that has been conveyed to take effect and be enjoyed after the termination of a prior estate, such as when an owner conveys a life estate to one party and the remainder to another.

Secured debt A debt on which the borrower pledges collateral as security for future payment of the debt.

Selling expenses All expenses incurred to complete the sales transaction. If a capital gain is realized on the sale, the selling expenses reduce that gain.

Selling/Purchase price For tax purposes, the amount realized on a sale, including the amount of cash received plus the fair market value of any other property received.

Time-share A form of ownership interest that may include an estate interest in property and which allows use of the property for a fixed or variable time period.